Collins

need to know?

Riding

The British Horse Society

The British Horse Society
Registered Charity No. 210504

Margaret Linington-Payne

Collins

First published in 2007 by
Collins, an imprint of
HarperCollins Publishers
77–85 Fulham Palace Road
Hammersmith, London W6 8JB

The Collins website address is:
www.collins.co.uk

Collins is a registered trademark of HarperCollins Publishers Limited

11 10 09 08 07

6 5 4 3 2 1

The British Horse Society is a registered charity (no. 210504)
The British Horse Society website is: www.bhs.org.uk

A catalogue record for this book is available from the British Library.

Created by: **SP Creative Design**
Editor: **Heather Thomas**
Designer: **Rolando Ugolini**

Photography
All photography by **Rolando Ugolini** with the exception of the following:
Margaret Linington-Payne: pages 29-31, 98–99

Based on material from *The British Horse Society Complete Horse and Pony
Care (Collins)*

ISBN: 978-0-00-725517-7
Printed and bound by **Printing Express Ltd, Hong Kong**

Contents

The British Horse Society

The British Horse Society was founded in 1947 to work for the good of horses and riders. Membership now stands at almost 65,000. In addition, there are 38,000 members of affiliated Riding Clubs. The Society's charitable objectives are to promote the welfare, care and use of horses and ponies.

must know

Off-road routes
The Society is involved with the additions of promoted off-road routes. All these routes are key initiatives of the Ride-UK project, which was launched by The BHS in 2000 with the vision of creating a network of riding and driving routes throughout the UK.

Access and rights of way

The Society's network of over 170 Bridleway Officers and 130 Affiliated Bridleway Groups targets rural and urban access. The BHS is in consultation with Highway Authorities and other access organizations. The DEFRA (Department for Environment, Food & Rural Affairs) commissioned British Horse Industry Strategy aims to increase access to off-road riding and carriage driving. The BHS Access Department is working hard to achieve this, together with its partners in the Equestrian Access Forum.

Breeding and welfare

Breeding and welfare is another important aspect of The BHS's work. To prevent neglect and cruelty, the Society educates and advises horse owners, especially new ones, on correct management practices. Over 90 BHS county Welfare representatives support and advise owners throughout the country. BHS Welfare represents over 40 breed societies affiliated to The BHS Horse and Pony Breeds committee. Active BHS participation on the National Equine Welfare Council, DEFRA sub-committee meetings and Horserace Betting Levy Board committee meetings helps ensure the future wellbeing of horses in the UK.

Safety

The BHS Safety Department is involved in every aspect of equestrian safety, representing all riders. The Society works closely with the Department for Transport and, as a result of their campaigning, the Highway Code includes specific advice to all who take horses on the road. Work with the County Surveyors Society has led to joint guidance being issued to Highway Authorities. The BHS Riding & Road Safety Tests take place throughout the UK and Eire with 4,500 people each year learning to ride safely on the roads. Information is available on safe equipment for horses and riders, with representation from The Society on many committees, including BSI and BETA. Working closely with other safety-related organizations, the Safety Department ensures that no aspect of equestrian safety is overlooked.

Training and education

The Training and Education Department administers a wide range of examinations, ranging from Progressive Riding Tests for recreational riders through to a full professional qualification structure. Qualified instructors work to ensure that horses are trained and ridden sympathetically. The BHS believes the public should be able to expect a high standard of teaching and safety from riding instructors, and it has created a Register of Instructors to meet this need. Since 1961, The BHS has run a scheme for the Approval of Riding Schools. There are approximately 950 BHS approved riding establishments in Britain and abroad. There is also an approved livery yard scheme to encourage livery yards to set high standards for their clients.

1 Choosing a riding school

Now that you have made the decision that you want to learn to ride or to pick up the skill again, you need to find a riding school that will suit your requirements. Riding schools vary greatly in their size, location and the facilities that they offer. In the UK, all riding schools have to hold a Local Authority licence, and this is the first thing you need to check.

Finding a riding school

If you choose a BHS Approved Riding School, you are guaranteed that the establishment holds the necessary licence, maintains high standards of instruction, horse care, health and safety, and has the statutory insurance covers. For more information on finding one, look on their website (see page 187).

Your goals

Before you start, you need to decide on what your goals are for your riding and what you want to get out of it. If you want to become competent enough just to hack out safely and to enjoy the countryside, then you should consider carefully whether it is worth starting to learn to ride at a riding school where they do not hack out, as you will have to move on once you are a more competent rider. On the other hand, however, a riding school that concentrates solely on instruction may get you up to your required standard more quickly.

Visit before you book

Your nearest riding school may not be the right one for you, so you must be prepared to telephone a few different centres before you make a visit. An initial phone call will give you a good idea as to whether a particular riding school has the potential to fulfil all your requirements and how customer-friendly the staff are. It is also very important for you to visit the centre and to have a look around to get the feel of the establishment and discuss your needs before booking your first lesson. So even if it sounds ideal over the telephone, do go and have a look.

must know

Points to look for
• The staff should be welcoming and friendly. They must be prepared to show you around and, if possible, let you watch a lesson in progress.
• All areas of the stable yard should be clean, neat and tidy.
• The horses should look well groomed, healthy and content.
• The atmosphere should be welcoming and there should be an air of efficiency about the place generally.

What to ask

Do not be afraid to ask the staff questions about the riding school's organization of riding lessons and how they like to assess potential new clients. You will need to feel comfortable about coming to the riding establishment, and confident that the staff will have your best interests at heart.

Ask about the qualifications that the staff have. The Preliminary Teaching test is the first BHS teaching qualification whereby members of staff are allowed to teach entirely by themselves. Teachers with this qualification may be newly qualified or could be very experienced indeed but have chosen not to progress further up the qualifications ladder.

Choosing an instructor

You will need an instructor who will be sympathetic to your needs and who can adapt their coaching methods to suit you and your goals. In addition, they need to be understanding of the fact that you

Even at a really busy riding school, the horses and ponies will be well cared for, and health and safety will be a priority.

A well-run riding school will make sure that all the areas, including riding surfaces, are maintained to the highest standards. Surfaces should be flat and never dusty.

must know

Indoor schools
Not all riding schools
have an indoor school.
This will not affect the
quality of instruction,
but it may influence
whether or not you will
want to ride regularly,
whatever the weather!

may not be able to achieve a classically correct
riding position, no matter how hard you try.

Many mature people who are learning to ride do
not feel comfortable being taught by someone who
is much younger than themselves. If you feel like
this, you must mention it on your first visit to the
riding school. If you are to succeed with your riding,
you will need to have confidence in the person who
is teaching you. If there is no trust, you will not
be able to relax and your progress as a rider will
be hampered. If, when you have had two or three
lessons, you still do not feel that you are achieving
a rapport with your instructor, discuss this with the
relevant person. There is no embarrassment in not
being able to get on with an instructor, so if you
highlight this and discuss the reasons why you feel
this way, the riding school may well be able to
change your teacher.

The horses in a riding school
should appear alert but well-
mannered, and their stables
should always be clean and tidy.

What to look for

Look at the horses, stables and paddocks while you are being shown round the yard, and take notice of how friendly and alert the horses appear. There may be one or two who are not as friendly as others, but generally they should seem relaxed and inquisitive. Always ask if it is acceptable to stroke them, and please do not offer them titbits over the door. If every visitor to the stables feeds the horses, it leads to them looking for food, biting, and kicking the doors. Consequently, many riding schools have a rule that horses may not be fed any titbits. A carrot given to a member of staff to be put into a horse's evening feed may be an acceptable compromise.

Look over the stable doors and check whether the horses' beds are clean and tidy. There are many different forms of bedding available for horses, but they should all be regularly 'skepped out', i.e. the droppings are taken out throughout the day.

Riding lessons, whether they are taken in an indoor or an outdoor school, should always be well structured, enjoyable and interesting as well as safe.

Many novice riders feel safer if they start to learn on the lead rein. The close proximity of a teacher can give you confidence and lead to quicker progress.

Fields and fencing

In some riding schools, the horses and ponies live outside in the fields when they are not working, although they may well be tied up in stalls when they are waiting to work. This is acceptable as long as the horses cannot reach each other to kick and bite. Always take note of how well maintained the fences and fields are when you are being shown round. Any fences should be secure and safe, and fields should not have noticeable areas of droppings which are left to rot down, nor should there be large amounts of weeds in well-maintained paddocks. As with the stable yard itself, everything outside should appear safe and well cared for.

This field is better maintained than the one shown opposite, as there are fewer weeds, and it is also securely enclosed with safe post and rail fencing.

Is expensive best?

On your first visit to any riding school, you will also need to discuss the cost of having different types of lessons. These can vary a great deal, depending on the riding school's location, overheads, staff costs and the facilities that are offered. The cheapest schools may not always be the best, but, on the other hand, the most expensive may not be either! You need to decide on what budget you have available and then choose the riding school that you feel will suit you best within that price range.

Although these horses look happy, healthy and generally well groomed, there are lots of weeds which need to be kept under control to ensure quality grazing.

Booking your first lesson

Now that you have decided on a riding school that has the right facilities for you, take the plunge and book your first lesson. There are several ways of doing this, and the route you choose will depend on your preferences and what you can afford.

When you feel more confident as a rider, some lunge lessons will ensure that you progress quite quickly. You will not only work harder than on the lead rein but you can also concentrate on improving your riding position.

Private lessons

The first option is to have private lessons. These are probably the quickest and easiest way to learn to ride, but they can be expensive. You will have a teacher on a one-to-one basis and will be given individual assistance. For your first few lessons, it is a good idea to book 30-minute sessions, so your body does not get tired nor your mind overloaded with too much new information. The best way to start if you are a complete beginner is to be led

around the school, either by the instructor or by an assistant. However, as your confidence grows, you will be able to take more control of the horse.

Lunge lessons

In a lunge lesson, the teacher attaches the horse to a long line and stands fairly still while the horse makes a circle round them. They also hold a long whip to encourage the horse to move forward. This kind of work is very hard, both for the horse and the rider, so a half-hour lesson is usually the maximum. Once you have gained some confidence sitting on a horse, a series of lunge lessons will help you to progress quickly with your position, balance and skill.

A lead rein lesson means that you do not have to worry too much about controlling your horse. Note the neckstrap around the horse's neck, so that you can hold on if you feel unsafe, without balancing on the horse's mouth.

Class lessons

Some schools may suggest joining a class lesson when you start learning. The advantage of learning this way is you can see that everybody else is having the same problems and can share the experience. Another benefit is that the concentration involved is not so great as in an individual one-to-one lesson.

Group lessons are usually of one hour's duration, and the number of people can vary – anything from three to about eight riders. The smaller the group, the more attention you will receive from your teacher.

If you are returning to riding after a long break, then the riding school may suggest a few individual lessons to brush up your basic skills before joining a group lesson at an appropriate level. If you are a complete beginner, however, you may wish to take a number of private lessons until you start to feel confident as a rider, and then move into a group session with other people.

want to know more?

- For a comprehensive list of BHS approved riding schools, go to www.bhs.org.uk
- Alternatively, you can obtain a publication from the British Horse Society entitled *Where to Ride and Train*. Ring 01926 707700.
- Further details can be obtained from the BHS Approvals office on 01926 707794, or email approvals@bhs.org.uk

2 Preparing to ride

Riding is a great way to take exercise, make some new friends and see the countryside. Now that you have taken the plunge and decided to have some lessons, you will need to ensure that you are safely equipped. You will also find that the fitter you are, the easier your lessons will be and the quicker you will progress. This chapter contains essential advice on getting ready to ride.

2 Preparing to ride

Clothing

When you have your first riding lessons, you may not want to go to the expense of purchasing all the clothing and equipment you will require straight away. It is usually better to wait a little while until you are sure that riding is the right sport for you and that you want to progress further.

must know

Help is at hand
The riding school will be willing to offer you help and advice about what is suitable to wear whilst not compromising your safety and comfort.

Riding hats

Most riding schools will have some riding hats for hire, which must conform to the current BSI (British Standards Institute) standards. However, it is always advisable to purchase your own riding hat after you have taken a few riding lessons.

To buy a hat, go to a tack shop that has its own registered hat fitter on the premises. They will ensure that you purchase a hat that not only fits you correctly but also offers your head the maximum amount of protection should you happen to take a fall. If you feel that in the future you may want to compete in one of the many riding disciplines that are now on offer, you should check first with the rules of that discipline to see what their special requirements are regarding hats.

Replacing hats

If you are unlucky enough to fall off your horse and land on your hat, it is always sensible to replace it as you can never be sure exactly how much damage the hat has incurred on impact. Continuing to wear it because it seems to be undamaged is a false economy; it is better not to compromise your safety just for the sake of the price of a new hat.

The chin strap of this hat is far too loose and is unsafe for the rider.

This hat is at an angle and therefore will not protect the rider's head in a fall.

This hat is sitting too far back on the rider's head and will not give protection.

This riding hat fits the rider well. Notice how it is positioned correctly on her head.

This horse is ideal for lunge lessons. He is a sturdy cob who looks sensible and is keen to do his job. The rider is appropriately dressed for a hot day.

Styles of riding hat

Riding hats are now available in two extremely distinctive styles: traditional velvet hard hats (see page 21 and above) and skull caps (see page 25), which are usually covered with a colourful silk or a velvet covering. Which type of hat is best for you? Well, generally, there is no difference in the amount of protection that both types of riding hat offer you as a rider, and which style you choose is really a matter of personal preference rather than safety. For cross-country riding, however, most people tend to favour the skull cap type of hat.

BSI standards

Always check the BSI standards inside the hat before buying. If you are unsure whether a hat is the right size for you, ask the staff in the store for advice.

Jodhpurs and breeches

For your first few riding lessons, you can wear some comfortable trousers rather than investing in a pair of jodhpurs. However, the trousers should not be too loose and baggy, or they will cause friction. On the other hand, if they are too tight, then there is a possibility of them splitting when you mount and sit astride the horse! Do not wear jeans because the seam on the inside is bulky and will chaff your legs.

Once you have decided that riding is definitely right for you, it is sensible to purchase a pair of jodhpurs, which are designed specifically for riding. They are not only comfortable to wear but will also protect your legs. Alternatively, you can wear breeches, but these are shorter than jodhpurs as they are always worn with long riding boots. They are also much more expensive than jodhpurs.

Jumpers and jackets

You need to wear clothing on your upper body that is suitable for the conditions in which you will be riding. It is always wise to keep your arms covered, so that if you are unfortunate enough to fall off they will be protected. However, many people do wear short-sleeved tops in summer if the weather is very hot. Do make sure that your clothes are not loose and flapping around as this may frighten the horse. A warm jumper in winter and a long-sleeved shirt in summer will fit the bill.

must know

Gloves
Riders are always advised to wear gloves, preferably close-fitting ones. They will not only protect your hands from the reins, preventing rubbing, but will also help to keep them warm in the winter.

You may need to wear a jacket or coat if you are riding outside or throughout the winter months. Always make sure that it is the right length, so you don't keep sitting on it, which can be extremely frustrating when you are riding.

Footwear

The correct footwear is an essential part of your equipment, and not only for riding. Horses are not aware of where you are putting your feet when you lead them, and thus they may inadvertently tread on one of your feet should you not be in the correct position. Therefore you always need to wear strong footwear that will provide you with some protection at all times.

Unsuitable footwear

Trainers are totally unsuitable and unsafe as they give no protection to your feet and have no heel. A small heel is crucial as it will stop your feet from slipping through the front of the stirrup should anything untoward occur. Heavy-ridged soles are also not suitable – they can trap your foot in the stirrup. If the tread is very deep, then it is hard to control your foot in the stirrup.

Which boots are best?

The ideal footwear for riding is a pair of jodhpur boots or long riding boots. You probably will not want to purchase these straight away, so a strong pair of shoes is a sensible substitute for your first few riding lessons. Lace-up shoes are better than those with buckles, which can catch on the stirrups. The sole of the shoe should not be too thick.

When you decide to purchase a pair of boots for riding, it is down to your personal preference whether you choose to wear short jodhpur or long riding boots. Long boots do offer more protection for your legs and can stop stirrup leathers chaffing and pinching. They come in leather and rubber; rubber ones are more affordable and are totally acceptable for leisure riders.

This novice is ill equipped for a lesson; a safety-conscious school would not allow him to ride. His trousers are too baggy and he is wearing trainers. He has a riding hat but it is set too far back on his head, and he has no gloves.

Get fit for riding

Riding is a sport and, although you do not need to be very fit to go out for a trek or a gentle hack in the countryside, if you want to progress with your skills, you do need to consider your level of fitness and the muscles you use the most when riding.

Use your muscles

Many people who are just starting to learn to ride are under the misapprehension that all you have to do to ride is just to sit on a horse. However, nothing could be further from the truth. Riding is a very healthy activity, which helps you use a large number of muscles in your body and this is why you may feel a little stiff or sore after your first few lessons. The fitter and more supple you are, the fewer problems you will experience, although a favourite saying of many riding teachers is: 'No pain, no gain!'

The exercises

There is a wide variety of exercises that you can undertake to help you to develop your suppleness and thereby make your riding lessons easier and more worthwhile. Initially, you may feel very stiff and unable to perform the exercises easily. Don't give up – if you can find just a small amount of time each day to practise them, you will gradually become more supple and this will really help you when you start to ride. Do not try to push yourself too hard too quickly, or you could do yourself real damage. If you are in any doubt about your general health or level of fitness, then you should consult a medical practitioner before starting.

must know

Starting off
If you are unaccustomed to exercising, it may be worth contacting your GP before you embark on any kind of exercise programme to discuss the best way of starting to get fit.

1 Standing up straight with your weight distributed evenly across both your feet, turn your head as far as you can to the left. Hold for up to 10 seconds, then look to the front.

2 Now repeat the exercise to the right. Check that you can turn your head the same distance in both directions – left and right. If one way is easier, then work more on the stiffer side.

1 This exercise improves flexibility and loosens your spine. Stand with your feet slightly apart, stretch your arms out at shoulder height and then twist as far as you can to the right.

2 Without moving your feet, twist as far as you can to the left. Repeat this exercise several times, working hard in order to achieve an equal rotation in both directions.

1 This exercise helps the triceps muscles and it can be done sitting or standing. Take your right arm up and then drop your hand down behind your head between the shoulder blades.

2 Take your left arm around your head and hold your right elbow. Hold like this for up to 10 seconds and then repeat the exercise on the other side with the left arm.

This is excellent for stretching out your calf muscles. Place your hands on a wall and take your left leg back. Lean your body weight on the wall and then hold for up to 15 seconds. Repeat with the other leg.

To stretch your inner thighs, sit up with your legs straight. Make fists with your hands and place them on the floor behind you. Open your legs, lean forward slightly and push down on your fists. Hold for 20 seconds.

1 This exercise helps to make the hip flexor muscles more supple. Kneel on one knee and stretch up tall, with your arms above your head. Hold for up to 10 seconds.

2 Now lean forward and rest your fingertips on the floor. Hold for up to 10 seconds and then return to the original position. Repeat with the other knee in the same way.

To aid core stability, sit on a Swiss ball with your weight equally distributed across both your seat bones.

Here the rider has more of her weight on the right seat bone. You can see how her shoulders are not level.

The rider has collapsed her left hip and slipped to the right, putting more weight on the left seat bone.

If you sit with your weight distributed properly, you should feel both your seat bones equally. Your shoulders and your hands should be at the same height.

A Swiss ball can help your core stability and balance. In a good position, your shoulders should be relaxed with your head directly above your spine.

What are your aims?

The fitter and more supple you are before you start
riding, the quicker you will progress. It really is
worth making the effort to work on your fitness
before you actually start to ride, although, of course,
it all depends on what you want from your riding
experience and how far you wish to go.

Now that you have made the decision to take
some lessons, sit down and ask yourself: 'What are
my expectations from learning to ride? What do I
want to get out of it?' You may not recognize your
long-term goals at the beginning, and these may
well change as you progress and find the sport
increasingly absorbing.

What may start as a desire to accompany a friend
or a sibling may turn into an overpowering passion
to learn more and even to become a competitive
rider. You may even start off just wanting to be able
to hack out on a sunny day but end up deciding that
you wish to make a career out of horses.

Riding in a classical position

To enjoy your lessons and riding experience you
need to have both long- and short-term goals. You
should discuss these with your riding instructor;
what you hope to achieve could alter the way in
which you will be taught. It is always better to try
and learn to ride in a classical position as near as
you possibly can. The reason for this is that from
a correct classical position, you can move on to
most other equestrian disciplines and your horse
will be able to work more easily for you.

If, however, you know for certain that you will
only ever want to have a quiet hack out, then it is

not so vital that your riding position is totally correct. You must, however, always be in balance with your horse and not have to use your reins to stay on board. To be balanced, your weight must be, as near as possible, over the horse's centre of movement, so that he can carry you easily. You will learn about this in the following chapters.

Riding out on a warm, sunny day is an enjoyable and exhilarating experience. Both the horse and rider look happy here.

Contact with horses

It is a good idea to spend some time with horses before starting to learn to ride. If you have ridden in the past, no matter how long ago, you will probably already have a little 'feel' for horses and will not be so worried about coming into contact with them.

Confidence is important

People who have no previous experience of horses may even find their size and behaviour intimidating. Consequently, if you can spend just a few minutes with them – perhaps stroking them over a stable door, or watching other people ride or look after them – you will be a little more confident when you finally start riding. Horses are large animals and some anxiety is perfectly normal if you are not accustomed to being around them. Any contact you can have with them will help to overcome this fear.

Approaching a horse

Because horses in the wild are animals of flight they can be nervous. If they are approached by someone making quick, sharp movements, they will become more nervous themselves. If you can approach them calmly and confidently, this will ensure that you get off to a good start with your mount.

You can only achieve this, however, if you have a certain degree of confidence yourself. This will come with familiarity, so take every opportunity to approach a horse and try to make friends with him. If you are unsure of how a horse behaves, it is safer to do this from the outside of the stable door and not to go into his stable. Do not try to do this in a

This horse and rider are showing mutual trust. The horse is happy and inquisitive, and the rider is positive but non-threatening.

field; you could end up putting yourself in a tricky position without even knowing it.

Observe and learn

If you get the opportunity, observe people who are confident with and knowledgeable about horses. Notice how they are always positive and purposeful when attending to a horse. Familiarity should never breed contempt when dealing with horses – they have brains and can think for themselves.

Most riding school horses will be sensible, well-mannered and accustomed to having people around them who are unsure of the environment, but this does not mean that you can be complacent. Horses should always be treated with kindness and respect to encourage the growth of a positive relationship between the rider and horse. It will certainly be worthwhile and the respect will be mutual.

want to know more?

• Read one of the books available on how horses think and behave. Start with the *The British Horse Society Complete Horse and Pony Care* (Collins).
• Visit your local tack shop and get the advice of a qualified hat fitter to find a riding hat that fits you properly and conforms to BSI (British Standards Institute) standards.

3 Your first lesson

The day has arrived for your first lesson, and if you have done your homework and chosen a riding school you feel confident about, then all should go well. Be prepared to listen to what you are being taught, and don't rush; take everything one step at a time. Horses are kind, helpful creatures who will do their best to accommodate you and will forgive your mistakes. Remember that you are taking up riding for fun, so relax and enjoy yourself.

How a horse thinks

For your first riding lessons, your horse may well be brought to the arena for you, but if you tell the staff at the riding school that you are keen to get to know your horse better, they should show you how to approach him and lead him yourself.

Stabling horses removes the opportunity for physical contact with other horses. Here the horses can at least see each other. A good school will turn out their horses regularly, for exercise and social contact.

Looking after a horse

Eventually, you should learn how to look after a horse, including some basic stable management skills, which are always useful. This helps you to start to understand the way in which a horse thinks, so that both of you will be safer together. Also, if you decide one day to take the huge leap and buy your own horse, you will need to know what skills are required to take care of him.

Horses in the wild

In the wild, the horse is a creature of prey, which means that he is constantly on the look-out for predators. Although he has excellent vision to the front and sides, there is a small area immediately in front of his head where he is unable to see.

As a creature of flight, the horse uses his speed to get him out of trouble. Only when he is cornered and there is no escape will he fight, using his legs and teeth to good effect to protect himself.

Wild horses travel in herds for safety, forming bonds with each other. Within the herd, there is a hierarchy and every horse knows his place within it. A horse may sometimes challenge this pecking order and may even succeed in raising his status within the herd.

You may think that all this has no relevance to learning to ride, but you need some knowledge of a horse's natural lifestyle and the way in which we compromise this when we domesticate him, so that you can understand better his reactions to what he is being asked to do.

This horse is showing a relaxed interest in his surroundings. He is not at all frightened and he appears to be quite confident with a good temperament.

Horses are herd animals and feel safer in the company of others. They will only relax and graze if they are not afraid, although one horse will be on guard.

Building a relationship

When we ride, we must remember that in the wild a weight on a horse's back means he has been attacked by a predator. Building up good relationships with horses by consistent handling and schooling means they gain our trust and are prepared to accept us humans as dominant, looking to us for support and guidance.

Always take the opportunity to talk to your horse and pat him before you mount.

Opposite: There is no better feeling than riding across open country on a well-schooled horse on a fine day. Riding with a friend is enjoyable and a good stress-buster after a hard day's work.

Starting to ride

When you have your first lessons you will be given a horse who is frequently used for novice riders. He will be able to help you out because he knows what is going to be asked of him, and he is not overly sensitive. The relationship you build up with your first horse is one you will never forget. Therefore it is important that for the first few lessons you are always given the same horse, so you can get used to his rhythm and obedience to the aids. You will then quickly become more confident and make progress.

One thing you will quickly learn about riding is that every horse is different, and therefore riders continually learn to adapt and refine their skills. Even the best riders in the world are still learning – the process never ends! So you must be patient and keep on practising – you will improve.

Some horses seem to sense what you want before you ask them while others take more persuasion. Just as with people, you will feel more comfortable with some horses than others. Learning to ride correctly is a long and sometimes bumpy road, but the rewards can be fantastic. You may even find yourself becoming obsessed with the desire to learn more as you continue to improve as a rider.

Points of the horse

Try to learn the 'points of the horse'. Your instructor may mention the withers or hocks, for example, and you should know where they are located on the horse. Spend some time looking at the points and try to familiarize them; it will be time well spent.

A healthy horse

A healthy horse's coat should appear shiny. His eyes should be bright and he should be alert and interested in what is going on around him. His ears should be facing forward, not pointing back. He should not be too fat nor too thin. This horse has all these traits and is well cared for.

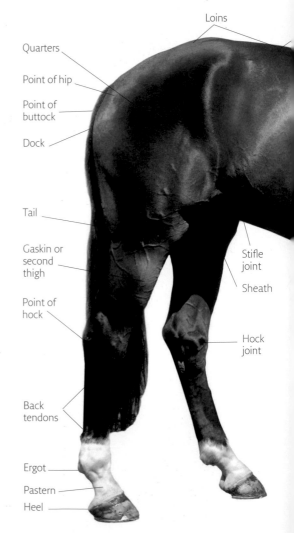

Loins
Quarters
Point of hip
Point of buttock
Dock
Tail
Gaskin or second thigh
Point of hock
Back tendons
Ergot
Pastern
Heel
Stifle joint
Sheath
Hock joint

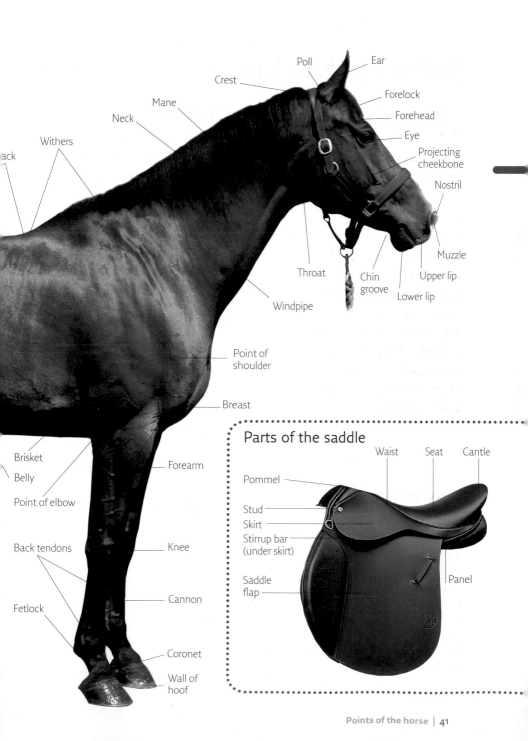

Poll

Ear

Crest

Forelock

Mane

Forehead

Neck

Eye

Withers

Projecting
cheekbone

ack

Nostril

Muzzle

Throat

Chin
groove

Upper lip

Lower lip

Windpipe

Point of
shoulder

Breast

Brisket

Belly

Forearm

Point of elbow

Back tendons

Knee

Fetlock

Cannon

Coronet

Wall of
hoof

Parts of the saddle

Waist

Seat

Cantle

Pommel

Stud

Skirt

Stirrup bar
(under skirt)

Saddle
flap

Panel

Leading a horse

The moment has finally come and you have arrived at the riding school for your first lesson. If you have already visited the school and booked the lesson in person, then you should have filled out the necessary paperwork. If not, you will be expected to do this before you mount and start to ride.

must know

Picking out the feet
A horse should always have his feet picked out before he comes out of the stable, so he does not drag his bedding onto the yard. This is not something you will be expected to do initially; it will be done by the person assisting you.

Leading out of a stable

If you are given the opportunity to lead the horse from his stable to the arena, there will be somebody there to help you and to ensure that everything is safe. You will be escorted into the horse's box and shown exactly what to do.

The horse will already be tacked up and will be tied up with a headcollar on over his bridle. The instructor who is with you will explain the particular routine for their riding school. The headcollar may well be undone at the horse's head and re-done up through the tie ring, or it may be untied at the wall, the headcollar then undone and taken out of the stable with the horse.

Leading guidelines

When leading a horse who is tacked up, always ensure that the stirrups are not flapping loose, so they cannot be caught on anything. Also, the reins should be taken quietly over the horse's ears, so that you have more to hold on to for security.

Traditionally the horse is led from his left side – the nearside. Horses should be encouraged to be led from both sides, but you will find it easier from the left. It is not a difficult procedure; just double

This rider is ready to mount. The reins are back over the horse's head and the stirrups have been pulled down in readiness.

When leading a horse, stand close to his shoulder and push him past you with a straight arm. This rider is safely positioned, but moving closer back towards the horse's shoulder will ensure she does not get her feet trodden on.

the reins up in your left hand, and with your right hand hold both reins behind the horse's chin. The only exception to this is if the horse is wearing a running martingale (see page 185), in which case you should not put the reins over his head as the martingale will pull down on his mouth.

This horse is being led out of his stall. Note how he is positioned in the centre of the doorway (top), and the rider does not turn him until he has exited completely.

It is sensible to be prepared and already wearing your riding hat and gloves. Not only will you be safer but also your hands will be free to lead your horse. Don't forget to talk to him and reassure him.

Secure the stable door

When taking a horse from a stable, it is important that the stable door is fixed back securely so that it will not be caught by the wind and then knock into either of you. You must ensure that you bring the horse straight out through the middle of the door to prevent him catching himself on the door. Do not attempt to turn him until his whole body is out of the doorway or you will inadvertently catch his hips.

Be confident

Once you are out of the stable, you should walk purposefully towards the arena with your horse. Walk to the side of him by his shoulder. If you get in front of him or try to pull him, he will back off from you. Also, you are less likely to get your feet trodden on if you are at the side.

Try and push the horse past you with a straight arm and be prepared to encourage him verbally with a brisk 'Walk on'. If you show you are nervous or not practised at leading horses, he will not respond to you as well as if you give him confidence in your movements and tone of voice. The person who is assisting you may well be on the other side of him, ensuring that you are both safe.

Now you can see why your horse is often brought into the arena for you. To lead a horse well is a skill in itself, but one that is well worth learning so that you can start to build up a relationship with him.

Pre-mounting checks

Before mounting your horse, you should get into the routine of carrying out a few basic safety checks. These simple procedures involve checking that the girth is done up properly and that the stirrups are approximately the right length for you – neither too long nor too short. It is important to do this every time you ride.

Checking the girth

Before you mount, you will need to check the girth. To do this, always put your hand under the front of it. If you put your fingers under the back of the girth, you will be rubbing the horse's hair the wrong way and may make him uncomfortable.

The girth should feel firm to your hand; if not, you need to lift up the saddle flap and tighten the buckles. You will probably find that the two girth buckles are done up on the first and third buckle

1 Lift up the saddle flap in order to check the girth; you may need to adjust the buckles to tighten it.

2 Do make sure that both the buckles on the girth are tightened equally. Your teacher will check this, too.

3 Check how taut the girth is, and ensure that the buckle guard is pulled down over the buckles.

must know

Stirrup length
If you check your stirrup length before mounting, you will not have so much adjusting to do once you are mounted. You will be secure in the saddle even if a slight change in stirrup length needs to be undertaken.

straps. This is done for sound safety reasons – the first and second buckle straps are usually attached to the saddle by the same piece of webbing, and if the girth was attached to those and the webbing broke then you could experience a real problem. However, if they are attached to the first and third buckles and one piece of webbing breaks, you will still have one buckle attached.

By using two straps that are not positioned close together, it can also make everything less bulky under your thigh. Always ensure that you pull the buckle guard down over the buckles – this will also help to protect your leg.

Checking the stirrups

The next thing you have to do after checking the girth is to check the approximate length of your

After tightening the girth, always pull the 'buckle guard' down over the girth buckles. This will help to protect the saddle, and your leg from being rubbed by the buckles.

stirrups to ensure that they will not be far too long nor too short when you mount.

Adjusting the length

This is a simple procedure – all you need to do to alter the length of the stirrup is to pull down the buckle under the skirt of the saddle, take the tongue of the buckle out of the hole and then move the buckle up or down to make it shorter or longer. Your riding instructor will show you how to do this correctly. Once this is done, you need to pull down the underside of the leather until you hear the buckle click on the stirrup bar.

Of course, you must then go round to the other side of the horse, changing hands, and check the stirrup on the other side. Study the photographs below to see how to check the length of stirrups.

Above: This stirrup will probably be far too long for the rider when she is mounted. Notice how the leather has a loop in it.

Left: Note how the rider's stirrup iron just reaches her arm pit, so the stirrup will probably be about the correct length when she is mounted on her horse.

Mounting

The next major hurdle is to get on to your horse. Many schools encourage you to do this from a mounting block (see page 50), but it is a good idea to be able to mount from the ground, too.

(see page 50)

must know

From the ground
If you are mounting from the ground, once you have your left foot in the stirrup you need to spring once or twice on your right leg to give you momentum, then spring up, passing your right leg over the horse's quarters before sitting down in the saddle.

How to mount

If you mount from a block – which is easier for both you and your horse – you are more likely to mount efficiently, and there will be no damage to the saddle or the horse's back. However, most of the time, you will have to mount from the ground in the traditional way. If you have brought the horse into the arena yourself, the first thing to do is put the reins back over his ears. Put your arm through the reins, so that you have some control but leave both hands free. Your instructor will probably give you a demonstration of the correct way to mount. Whether you are mounting from a block or from the ground, the basic principles are the same.

Holding the reins

You need to take up your reins through the bottom of your left hand. Make sure the reins are not twisted and that they are not too long nor too short. If they are too short, there will be too much pressure on the horse's mouth and he will react by moving backwards or fidgeting. If they are too long, you will not be able to stop the horse from moving forwards while you are mounting.

1 With the reins through the bottom of your left hand, place it on your horse's neck. If using a mounting block, do not stand in such a way that you cannot see the horse's hindquarters.

2 With your right hand, take the back of the stirrup iron and bring it out towards you. Hold the stirrup iron, not the leather. The leather may look twisted but it will turn as you mount.

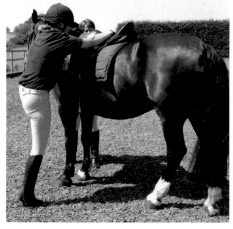

3 Put your left foot in the stirrup and push your toes down, so that you will not dig your horse in the ribs as you mount. Notice how this rider is just about to push her toes down.

4 Reach for the waist of the saddle on the off-side. Swing your right leg clear over your horse's quarters and sit down gently in the saddle. Try to make the movement quick but controlled.

must know

A 'leg up'
When you have been riding for some time, you may be offered a 'leg up'. This is a skill that you will learn later on; it is not easy for a novice rider to perform.

Mounting from a block

Horses have to get used to being mounted from a mounting block and feel happy to stand still and close enough for you to mount safely. Always make sure that you have checked the girth and stirrups (see pages 45–47) before approaching the block.

It is more beneficial for your horse's back if you mount him from a block, so you should not feel awkward or embarrassed about using one. Some people even feel that they have failed as a rider if they are unable to mount from the ground, but this is far from the truth.

The benefits for the horse and the saddle should always be your major consideration when you are mounting – not whether you feel foolish or less of a rider for having to use a mounting block.

1 Always make sure that the back part of the stirrup is turned outwards, in the same way as when you mount a horse from the ground.

2 When your left foot is in the stirrup, reach for the waist of the saddle and positively but gently push yourself up with your right leg.

3 Sit gently in the saddle with your weight evenly distributed. You must ensure that you and your horse are comfortable before setting off.

Check the girth again

It should become a habit once you are mounted to check your girth. Horses can learn the trick of puffing out their rib cage when you first do up the girth, and what felt tight before you mounted may now be rather loose, so make sure you check it again before moving off.

1 When you are mounted, check that the girth is correctly fastened. To do this, put both the reins into your right hand, lean down and put the fingers of your left hand under the girth near your horse's elbow. It should feel taut with no large gap between the horse and the girth.

2 If the girth feels loose, leaving your left foot in the stirrup, bring your leg up on to the horse's shoulder. Lift the saddle flap with your left hand and feel for the girth strap. Tighten both buckles, check that the buckle guard is in place and then let the flap fall back into place.

3 Finally, you can bring your leg back into the correct position. You will need to check your girth again after you have been riding for a few minutes. Although this skill appears to be relatively easy, in reality to keep your balance and feel safe will take a lot of practice.

Altering the stirrups

Once you are mounted, you may feel that your stirrups are not the correct length. To alter them when mounted is quite a difficult skill to master, so the sooner you start practising the better. Eventually it needs to be done by feel rather than by looking at what you are doing, but this comes only with practice. Your riding instructor may well alter your stirrups for you.

1 To alter your left stirrup, put the reins in your right hand. With your left hand, pull the spare piece of stirrup leather up towards you, so the tongue comes out of the hole.

2 To make the stirrup longer, push with your foot onto the iron. Let the leather slide down until comfortable. With your finger, feel the tongue of the buckle back into the nearest hole.

3 Now you can pull the underside piece of leather until you hear the click on the stirrup bar. This tells you that the buckle is as high as it can be.

4 Put the spare piece of leather behind your thigh, so that it will not rub or pinch the skin of your thigh. You are now mounted correctly and ready to move off.

Holding the reins

If you are a complete beginner, you may not even hold the reins for the first part of your lesson. Instead, you may be asked by your teacher to hold onto the neckstrap or the front of the saddle.

Light hands

If you do hold the reins, however, make sure that you hold one in each hand, so that they come up between your little and ring fingers, through the palm of your hand and out over the top of your index finger with your thumb pushed gently on the top. The spare end of the reins should be placed between the reins themselves and your horse's neck; this is to ensure that their weight does not press on to the rein and thereby be transmitted down to the horse's mouth.

Light and relaxed

Your hands should be in a position just above your horse's withers, 7.5–10cm (3–4in) apart, and they should be level. Your hands and wrists should feel light and relaxed. Try thinking of having a small bird in each hand which you don't want to squash to death but, equally, you don't want to fly away – this is the kind of feel that you are trying to maintain with your hands on the reins.

You can see that this is no easy task when you are a beginner and there are so many other things to think about, and this is why some riding schools suggest that you do not hold the reins initially. It is always important to remember that the horse's mouth is at the other end of the reins.

These reins are being held correctly. They come up between the little and ring fingers and through the palm of the rider's hand. The thumbs push gently on the reins to help stop them slipping.

This rider's hands are turned flat, so that the thumbs are not uppermost. You should avoid this as it makes for 'heavy hands' on the horse's mouth.

These reins are being held incorrectly. The part coming from the horse's mouth is going through the thumb and index finger, making 'heavy hands'.

Your riding position

Your instructor will probably demonstrate to you the position that you should try to achieve when you are riding your horse. It is generally accepted that the 'classical' riding position is best, and this is the one that is currently taught and used.

must know

What are the aids?
These are the methods used to control a horse. There are various ways to give him information as to what we want: natural and artificial.
• The natural aids are our seat, legs, hands and voice.
• The artificial aids are those we give with pieces of equipment. The most common are the various types of whip. You will not use artificial aids until you have good co-ordination and balance.

The classical riding position

It has the advantage that you sit over the horse's centre of motion, thereby making it easier and more comfortable for him to carry you. It also means that you can use all your riding 'aids' efficiently (see page 62) and, eventually, unobtrusively.

The 'invisible lines'

There are two invisible 'straight lines' in the classical riding position. The first is a line that goes down the side of your body from your ear, through your shoulder, hip and heel. The second is a line that runs from your elbow, down the bottom of your arm and hand, along the reins to the bit in the horse's mouth.

You should be sitting centrally in the lowest part of the saddle with your weight equally distributed on to your seat bones. Your stirrups must be of the same length so that you do not lean to one side.

Stay in balance

A horse is not an armchair and you should not sit slumped with your weight at the back of the saddle. Although this may be more comfortable for you, the rider, it is much more difficult for the horse to carry you as you are 'out of balance' with

The rider (left) is sitting 'square' with her weight distributed equally through both seat bones. In the picture above, the rider has collapsed her right hip and slipped left. Both she and the horse look uncomfortable.

him, i.e. your weight is not positioned correctly over his centre of motion.

Have you ever given somebody a piggy back? If they slip down your back, then your immediate reaction is to push them back up again, so that it becomes easier to carry them. However, the horse cannot do this if your weight slips back and he has to suffer in silence. This may give him a sore back and will certainly mean that he is unable to perform at his best for you.

must know

Practise, practise...
Even the basic skills can
be difficult to master
at first. Your instructor
will help you in the early
stages and will check
you have completed
the tasks safely. The old
adage that 'practice
makes perfect' is very
true, and soon you will
find that these tasks are
second nature to you.

It is also incorrect to tip forwards and let your
legs slip back when you are riding. This will put
you in a very insecure position, and if the horse
trips or moves suddenly, you will inevitable land on
the ground. You will also be unable to use your aids
(see page 56) efficiently.

Achieving a good position

A good riding position is something that we are
all trying to achieve and maintain. For many of
us, however, it will not be possible to master the
genuinely correct classical position, but for our
horses' sake we should continually try to do so, and
this is where the fitness exercises we perform off
the horse (see page 26) can really help to improve
our suppleness and thereby increase the likelihood
of us achieving the dizzy heights of a correct
classical position. You should make some time,
if possible, to practise them every day.

Here, the rider appears to be perched on top
of the horse. She is not balanced or relaxed
and she looks very insecure. If the horse trips,
she is more likely to fall off.

This rider is sitting too far back on the horse
with her feet pushed forwards. She may feel
comfortable, but it can give the horse a sore
back. It is more difficult for him to carry her.

What to expect

During your first riding lesson, you will probably spend a lot of time talking about your riding position and feeling the movement of your horse underneath you. You will probably be led round an indoor or outdoor arena on a leading rein and may stay in walk throughout. However, your instructor may give you the opportunity to try a sitting trot.

If you start off slowly and carefully, you will progress faster once you have established your basic riding position. Do not be afraid to ask your instructor any questions that come to mind, and do let them know if you are experiencing any problems, so that they can help to eliminate them.

Dismounting

At the end of the lesson, you will need to dismount correctly. To do this, you need to place both your reins in your left hand with a piece of the horse's mane. Take both your feet out of the stirrups, and then lean forwards and throw your right leg over your horse's bottom. Try to land on both feet, facing forwards, and keeping hold of the reins.

Your instructor will then show you how to run your stirrups up the back of the stirrup leathers. You are now ready to take the reins back over your horse's ears in readiness for leading him back to his stable. Remember what you have been taught – to lead him from his left side, walking by his shoulder with your feet well out of harm's way. Your first riding lesson is over and you have taken your initial steps towards becoming a rider. You should be exhilarated by the experience and feel that you have achieved something worthwhile.

want to know more?

- Although there is no substitute for practice when trying to improve, watching other riders will help you distinguish a good position from an incorrect one.
- The BHS bookshop stocks a wide range of specialist books that you can study. Look on the BHS website: www.britishhorse.com

4 The basics

Now that you have learnt the correct way to lead your horse, mount up, check the girth and alter the stirrups, the time has arrived when you can start using your aids to communicate with your horse. You can also learn how to start, turn and, most important of all, stop! To be able to co-ordinate your aids will take time and practice, but you will soon learn to use your seat, legs and hands to pass on your instructions to your horse.

The aids

When you start using your aids you may be a little uncoordinated, so communicating with your horse effectively could be difficult. The horse might not be sure as to what you require of him. He will probably sense that you are a novice rider and that you are anxious and uncertain about what is going on.

This rider is sitting in a basically correct classical position with her hands as a pair. A novice might find these stirrups a little long.

Opposite: This rider has her left rein shorter than her right. Therefore her hands are not a pair and her horse is looking left.

Using the aids

Always try to make your aids clear and positive, but not overly strong. It is better to use gentle aids first, and then, if your horse does not respond, you can be a little firmer. If you are too positive initially and your horse is very responsive, you may find yourself going faster than you want to.

Light hands

To become a good rider, you must work towards having sympathetic and light hands. Remember that at the other end of the reins you are holding a large lump of metal, which is in your horse's mouth.

Handling your reins

When you start riding, your reins frequently slip longer. However, this will happen less often as your riding improves and you maintain that gentle but firm feel on the reins that is so important (see page 54). As you become more relaxed, your arms will follow the movement of your horse more readily, so he will not take the reins from you. Because you will frequently lose 'contact' with the horse's mouth, you must become efficient at shortening your reins. The best way to do this is shown on page 64.

The same length

Make sure the reins are the same length. To do this correctly, you need to feel the weight that you have in each hand is the same, and that the tips of your horse's ears appear level in front of you. If they are not level, his head may be tilting and you will probably have one rein shorter than the other, pulling his head one way all the time. This will make it difficult for your horse to move forward correctly.

1 The reins are held correctly in both hands, but the rider feels the need to shorten them.

2 To shorten your left rein, put it through the thumb and first finger of the right hand.

3 Slide the left hand down the left rein until it is the length that you require.

4 Let go of the left rein with the right hand. To shorten the right rein, reverse the process.

5 Here the reins have been correctly shortened and the hands are positioned correctly.

Moving forward and halting

The first aid that you will learn is how to make your horse move forward from halt to walk. However, it is also very important for you to know how to slow down before you start moving off! This should give you more confidence.

Walking on

To ask your horse to walk on, 'take off the brakes'. To achieve this, you need to give a little with your hands towards the horse's mouth. However, do not exaggerate the movement – do just enough to release any pressure on the mouth.

Now think of sitting up tall and give your horse a gentle nudge with both your legs. Think of using the whole leg and not just the lower leg from the knee downwards.

must know

Your horse's mouth
Remember that you need a light touch. The bit at the end of the reins is in your horse's mouth, and you need to be sensitive when using your rein aids.

The rider shown here is using her legs correctly on the girth to ask her horse to move forward.

must know

Be relaxed
The head of a walking horse moves backwards and forwards. If your hands are light and not fixed, the horse will move them with this motion. This is good practice and shows you are relaxed. Your horse will feel he is not being restricted and he will be happy to keep walking forwards. Initially, you may not hold the reins in your hands, but when you feel safe enough to let go of the neckstrap or pommel, your hands should move to and fro with the horse's motion if you are relaxed.

Try to feel that your legs are staying in the same place near the girth to give this aid. It is far easier to move your legs back to do this, but this is incorrect and can make you tip forwards.

If your riding position does not have the straight line down the side of your body (see page 56) and your lower leg is pushed too far forwards, your leg will not come into contact with your horse's sides and the leg aid will not be clear to your horse.

Using your legs correctly

Later on, you will need to be able to use your legs further back to tell your horse to execute more complicated movements. To use your legs correctly is one of the most difficult manoeuvres for a novice rider. A good exercise is to place a football between your calves. Practise pushing your calves together to get the feel of the muscles that you need to use.

Notice how this rider has moved her legs too far back to use to ask her horse to walk on.

The halt

To ask your horse to stop is not at all difficult; just think of sitting up tall, and close your fingers round the reins and keep your legs on the horse's sides. If your reins are too long and your horse does not respond, then bring your hands back towards you, keeping the straight line with your arms and down the reins. This means that your hands come almost towards your stomach, and not down towards your horse's withers.

When you become a more competent rider and can keep a consistent rein contact, your hands will not need to move in a backward direction. It may seem strange initially to keep your legs on your horse's sides, but this will help him to step up with his hind legs into the halt.

This horse has halted squarely, with his weight distributed equally on all four legs. This means that you can only see two legs when looking from the side.

Turning your horse

Now that you have learnt how to make your horse start and stop by applying the correct aids, you also need to be able to get him to turn to the right or the left on command.

Opposite: This rider is learning how to ride in an arena. She will eventually be able to make her horse work round the outside and perform school figures.

Turning left

When you want to turn your horse to the left, the first thing you should do is to look to the left. As you do this, open your left hand. Turn your wrist a little as well, so that you think towards the movement that you would make with your thumb if you were, say, a hitchhiker thumbing a lift.

Your inside leg needs to nudge a little in its normal position near the girth. If you can remember to do it, your outside leg should move back behind the girth and also nudge a little. This outside leg movement will become increasingly important as you progress with your riding and wish to influence the horse more. However, as a novice rider, it may be one thing too many for you to think about at the moment. Don't worry if this is the case – you just need to be aware that later on this movement will become important.

Turning right

To get your horse to turn right is equally simple; all you need do is just repeat the instructions outlined above for turning left, but do them on the other side to the right. As your horse turns in the direction you require, you can gently release the aids back to the 'normal' position, so that he realizes you want him to go straight.

Walking

The walk is a four-time movement in which the horse puts one leg down at a time. The sequence of legs when he moves in walk is as follows: if he starts with the left hind leg, the left front leg will be the second beat, the right hind leg will be the third beat, and the right front leg will be the fourth beat.

must know

Changes of rein
Practise turns, halting and walking on until you feel confident and understand how light the aids can be for the horse you are riding. Some turns will involve 'changing the rein' in the arena, and there are many different changes of rein you can practise.

Feeling the movement

Walking is not difficult and, as you start to become more confident as a rider, you will begin to feel the movement of your horse's legs beneath you. This is something that you can start to think about as your confidence gradually increases and riding becomes a more natural process for you.

Improving your 'feel'

It is extremely important that you try to continually improve your 'feel' of the way in which your horse moves underneath you. This will not only help you with your general control but eventually will also mean that you can affect the work that your horse does, enabling you to help him improve the quality of his way of going.

Look at the shoulders

If you are unable to feel the horse's legs moving beneath you, just take a look at the horse's shoulders. As his shoulder moves back towards you, the front leg on that side is on the ground. Doing this will at least help you to start to get the feel of the front legs moving.

Walking sequence

In the walk, the horse's head moves backwards and forwards, and the rider's hands should follow this movement rather than block it, as shown in the photographic sequence below.

1 The right hind leg is coming forwards and is being put down to make the first beat.

2 The right fore leg is the next leg to move forwards and be placed on the ground.

3 The horse's left hind leg is now moving forwards to make the third beat.

4 The horse's left fore leg is brought forwards to complete the sequence.

Trotting

When you feel confident about asking your horse to walk on, turn and stop, you will be ready to learn to trot. There are two ways in which you can trot – rising and sitting.

must know

Rhythm of the trot
Think about the rhythm of the trot underneath you. Can you feel the one–two, one–two? If you can't, it is difficult to learn the rising trot, where you 'post' up and down in the saddle in time with the rhythm. Try saying 'one– two, one–two' out loud to ensure you feel the rhythm. Your teacher will tell you if you've done it correctly.

Feeling the movement

You should learn to do a small amount of sitting trot first, as it will give you the feel of the movement and will help you learn to rise. When the horse moves from walk to trot, the sequence of his legs changes from four beats to two. He does this by putting down diagonally opposite pairs of legs together with a moment of suspension in between (a short time when all four of his legs are off the ground).

Good posture

Good posture is essential if you want to become a first-class rider eventually. If you think of a skeleton, the spine is very slightly concave in the small of the back. This is how your spine should be when you adopt a good posture and, consequently, when you are out riding. You should always be aware of your posture, not only when you are riding your horse but also at different times of the day, such as when you are driving your car, sitting at a desk working in the office, relaxing at home or walking.

Improving your posture
You might even like to try the traditional way of improving your posture by walking around with a book on your head for a few minutes a day – it will certainly help you with your riding position.

Opposite: This rider is riding the trot across the long diagonal of the school. She is relaxed and is in good balance. Her horse is thinking forward and listening to her, waiting for the next aid.

Sitting trot

In the sequence of photographs below, the rider has undertaken three steps of sitting trot and then has started rising in the fourth image. When you start learning to trot, hold on to the neckstrap or the front of the saddle; then if you feel unsafe, you will not be tempted to pull up on the reins and affect the horse's mouth.

1 The right hind and left front legs (with blue bandages) are moving forward together.

2 The left hind and right front legs (with white bandages) are moving forward together.

3 The sequence is repeated, with the blue bandaged legs called the left diagonal pair.

4 This is followed by the white bandaged legs, which are known as the right diagonal pair.

This rider (left) is practising her sitting trot on the lunge. She is sitting tall but is relaxed.

Although this rider's stirrups are quite short (above), she is still sitting relatively tall and soft.

Notice how this rider is holding on to the horse's neckstrap to help her to balance.

The sitting trot

To sit correctly for a sitting trot, just think of sitting up tall, lifting your diaphragm a little and trying to stay as soft as you can through your hips. If you can achieve this, you will find that your horse will move you, and you will start to absorb the motion he gives you. If you can stay soft and relaxed, it will be much easier. Unfortunately, this is easier said than done, and many novice riders who feel a little anxious about learning to ride are consequently rather stiff. This means they are unable to absorb the movement and the process becomes more difficult, making them even stiffer. This is why you should practise your trot in short bursts, so that you can rest and readjust your position ready to try again. There is no secret in learning to ride; it is just practice, practice and good teaching.

The rising trot

To learn rising trot, you can start off by practising standing up and sitting down in the saddle in halt. Firstly, stand up and see if you can balance and stay there. The secret of this is to keep your lower leg secure and your whole leg as near as you can in a straight line. Although this exercise is good for your

1 This rider has her seat in the saddle. She is preparing to rise on the next beat.

2 She is rising up here, although her upper body could be inclined a little more forward.

3 The rider now sits down again. She has not let her leg push forward.

4 She now rises again. Her lower leg is secure but her hands are 'thinking' backwards.

balance, it is not the actual technique for use in the rising trot, as outlined below.

When you start to practise your rising and sitting (still in halt) try to think of your hips coming a little forward as you rise. You will not need to go as high as you did when you tried standing up. The secret is to try and control the coming down part and to sit softly down on to your seat bones and not to allow yourself to sit heavily on to the back of the saddle. If you do this, your lower leg will shoot forwards and you will be unable to continue to rise without pulling up on your hands.

To undertake the rising trot correctly is difficult and it needs a lot of practice. You will probably find initially that you will fall behind your horse's centre of balance. If this happens, ask the person who is in charge of your horse to walk, so that you can correct your position: bring your leg back under you and sit up correctly again. Do not worry if this takes you a long time, as it is better to get the technique correct at the beginning rather than having to relearn it later on. Once you are confident in executing the rising trot and do not have to use your hands to help you balance, you can start to use the reins and amalgamate the rising trot with control of your horse. Your riding skills are expanding already and are becoming easier to perform.

Correct technique

It is important to learn the correct technique for rising trot, so you can control your body and stay in rhythm with your horse. Resist the temptation of using your hands and reins to help you rise – your horse's mouth is at the other end of the reins.

This rider is happily riding in rising trot out on a hack. Riding on uneven ground can alter your horse's balance and rhythm and make rising trot more difficult.

want to know more?

• Watch other riders and see if you can spot their faults. Learn from their mistakes.
• For useful hints on trotting and other riding basics, read the monthly equestrian magazines:
Your Horse:
www.yourhorse.co.uk
Horse & Rider:
www.horseandrideruk.com
and *The Horse*:
www.thehorse.com

5 Progressing

Now that you are happy performing the rising
and sitting trot and are able to control your
horse in these paces, you can start to think
about adding some refinements. There is
always something new to learn in riding, and
just when you feel that you have reached a
level of competence in one skill, there will be
another thing that you need to master to help
improve your feel and riding ability. This
chapter gives you advice on how to progress.

Diagonals in rising trot

To make good progress as a rider, you now need to learn about your diagonals in rising trot. This name comes from the diagonal pairs of legs that your horse puts down as he trots.

Diagonal pairs

If you always sit on the same pair of legs your horse will start to brace himself for this and consequently will build up the muscles more on one side of his body than the other. You should sometimes sit on one diagonal pair of legs, and at other times on the other pair.

Fortunately, when we are riding in a school, we set a rule that says you should always do the sitting down part of the rising trot as your horse's outside front leg (and inside hind leg) are on the ground. This not only helps to balance the horse but also enables you to use your inside leg more easily to encourage him to use his inside hind leg.

When you are out hacking, there is no rule to be followed about which diagonal you are on. You should change frequently, however, so that you are not always rising on the same one.

Feeling the diagonals

Don't worry if you cannot feel yet which pair of legs is on the ground – as you make progress, this will come. For the moment, it may be easier just to look at your horse's outside shoulder, which comes back towards you as his front leg is on the ground.

1 The rider is on the right rein in the school and rising as the inside front leg is on the ground.

2 The rider then sits as the outside front leg is on the ground.

3 Look at the horse's leg bandages. The right diagonal pair are white and the left are blue.

4 The rider sits as the blue legs touch the ground and rises when the white legs are on the ground.

Consequently, if you are in sitting trot, you will see this shoulder coming back towards you and then you can start rising. This is one of the reasons why you should always start your rising trot with a few strides of sitting.

Some people find it difficult to work it out this way, so you could look at the inside shoulder and rise as that one is coming back towards you. It has the same result. If you keep looking to the inside, you can throw your weight too much this way and thus disrupt both your balance and that of your horse. It is more difficult to throw your weight too much to the outside.

The diagram below of a standard size arena shows some changes of rein you may be asked to make when riding in a school.

Changing the rein

If you think about it, you will be changing your diagonal frequently when you are riding in a school

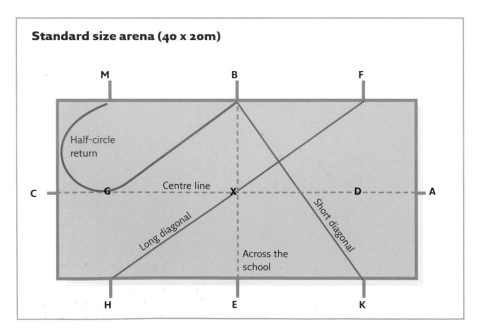

Standard size arena (40 x 20m)

M   B   F

Half-circle return

C — — G — — — Centre line — X — — — — D — — A

Long diagonal

Short diagonal

Across the school

H   E   K

as you will need to do it every time you change the rein. If you are going across the long diagonal, the best place to change the rein is just before you reach the letter you are going to. If, however, this is not convenient, then change it as soon as it is opportune.

must know

Wrong diagonal?
If you find yourself on the wrong diagonal, which can happen frequently, then you simply have to sit twice – or miss one up beat – and then you will be sitting on the correct diagonal (pair of legs).

The rider is sitting on the inside diagonal pair of legs and rising as the outside diagonal pair are on the ground. This is incorrect, and she needs to sit twice in order to change the diagonal.

Confidence

You may be thinking by now: 'Am I making progress quickly enough or in a similar way to other novices?' It is important to remember that everybody is an individual and what one person finds easy may be difficult for another, and vice versa.

Group lessons

If you are having private lessons and you now feel ready to move on, it may be worth talking to your instructor to find out if this would be a good time to move in to a group lesson. You will not receive personal tuition but you will see other riders having problems and be able to discuss all things equine with them. If you feel confident enough to make this step, then you are definitely making progress.

Build up gradually

Confidence is very important in learning to ride, and this is also true of your whole equine experience. If you are over-confident, it is tempting to try things beyond your limitations, which could lead to your downfall. However, if you have no confidence, you will progress very slowly and may even feel that riding is not for you. A good teacher will build up your confidence gradually to help you improve your riding skills – the two go hand-in-hand. Even the best riders in the world will sometimes have twinges in their confidence, so don't worry about that. Just work within your limits until you feel that a new task has become easy and almost 'second nature', and then you will be ready to move on to mastering more difficult skills.

Opposite: The rider (top) is riding the sitting down part of rising trot well, but her upper body should not incline further forwards. For the rising (below), she need not rise quite so high. Let the horse's movement push you out of the saddle, then go a little further and control the movement down.

Riding without stirrups

One skill we all need to learn – which is excellent for improving our balance, position and confidence – is riding without stirrups. Your instructor may introduce a small amount of this as soon as they feel you are confident enough to cope with it.

Walking without stirrups

If riding without stirrups is undertaken too early, there will be little benefit. If the prospect horrifies you to the point that you become so stiff you are unable to move, there is no advantage in trying it.

When you first ride without stirrups, however, you will only do it in walk. Once you take the plunge, you will probably feel that it is nowhere near as bad as you thought. Stirrups impose a discipline on your legs in order to keep them in the same place, and when you can get rid of them, you may find that you can soften your hips more easily.

In order to ride without stirrups, you will probably be asked by your instructor to 'quit and cross' them. As in most aspects of being around horses, there are accepted ways of doing things. The conventional method is shown opposite in more detail.

Starting in halt

Initially, when you quit and cross your stirrups, it is best to do it in halt, so that you do not have to worry about what the horse is doing and keeping in balance with him. Make sure that you keep a contact on the reins in case your horse does decide that he wants to move. If so, you will be able to restrain him quickly and effectively.

1 After you have taken your feet out of both the stirrups, you should pull down the buckles.

2 Next you must cross the right stirrup over your horse's withers on to his shoulder.

3 Now repeat the process with the left stirrup, so that the leathers are crossed over the withers.

4 If the buckle is turned upside down, the stirrup leather will lie flat under your thigh.

With stirrups, the rider's leg is short with the thigh at an angle of about 45 degrees to the hips. Compare this to the leg position without stirrups (right).

Without stirrups, you can see that the rider's thigh is longer and straighter, and is in a good position for flatwork.

Taking away your stirrups

To take away your stirrups, you must take both feet out and then pull the buckles down and away from the stirrup bar a short way. You can then put the stirrups over your horse's withers and rest them on the sides of his shoulders. Cross the right stirrup over first. You do this so that if you should happen to slip gracefully to the ground, you will only have one stirrup to uncross to remount. As you cross the stirrups over your horse's neck, turn the leather and buckle upside down so that they lie flat and will not rub your thighs.

Relax your legs

Riding without stirrups is a good way to improve your riding position and feel. If you do feel unsafe at first, hold the neckstrap or front of the saddle with one hand and ask your instructor to lead you until you feel safer. Try to relax through your hips and let your legs feel long under you. Think of bringing your leg back from the hip so that your thigh is as long and straight as possible. One of the reasons you should ride without stirrups is to lengthen your leg, and the only way you can do this is by straightening your thigh. So if you grip with your thigh and fix your hips, this is of no benefit. Bring your thigh back from the hip and then let your leg hang down.

After working without stirrups, the rider is able to lengthen her stirrups in order to ride in a more classical position.

Reaching down towards your toes is a good exercise for stretching out your hamstrings.

Some relaxing leg exercises

• When mounted, circle your ankles both inwards and outwards – both legs together, then one leg at a time. This helps develop co-ordination and is good preparation for more advanced riding skills. Later on, you will have to do one thing with one leg and something else with the other – not easy when there is a horse underneath you.

• A good exercise, but one that you should be careful about trying, is to bring your leg out to the side a little and then back from the hip and let it relax. At first, only do this a small amount – it really pulls at your hip joint and may well give you cramp. To help do this when you are mounted, practise the exercise shown below on the ground.

1 Holding on to something for balance, bend one knee and lift your leg up as shown.

2 Slowly turn your knee out to the side, as far as it will go, but make sure you keep it high.

3 Lower the leg to the ground with the toes facing out, then repeat with the other leg.

Loosen your hips

To become a proficient rider with a riding position that makes it easier for the horse to carry you and for you to give subtle aids, it is important to loosen and soften your hips. The more mature we become, the stiffer we are in the hips, so we must work hard at this. You don't need the suppleness of a gymnast to be a good rider, but the softer you are in the hips, the easier it will be for you to ride well.

Feel the movement

When you ride without stirrups, you may feel the horse's movement underneath you more than you do when riding with them. Relax and just let the horse move you. Don't try to fix and push your hips with his movement. Sit tall with good posture (see page 72), and after a while it will not feel so bad; you might even enjoy it. You should feel that your hips and the small of your back are absorbing the horse's movement. And do keep checking that your hips and thighs are not tightening up.

Trotting without stirrups

Once you feel confident about walking without stirrups, you are ready to progress to trying a sitting trot without them, but just a few strides at first. Hold the neckstrap or the front of the saddle, so that you are not tempted to pull on the horse's mouth. There are several ways in which you can do this, and your teacher will advise you which one is best, depending on your own level of riding ability and confidence.

You could hold the reins in one hand and the point of contact with the other, or you could loosen the reins but keep hold of them both, with both hands holding the point of contact. Alternatively, you could be asked to let go of them altogether. If so, a knot will be tied in them and you can use your hands just for holding the point of contact.

Don't worry – your instructor will usually be close to hand and you will trot no more than a few strides. Try to sit up tall and let your horse move you. You may find that your position slips a little, but as soon as you walk, re-arrange yourself to correct it. It is much better to do several short trots where you can put yourself back into the correct position than to attempt a longer trot where your position just keeps on deteriorating.

If this rider had stirrups, the leathers would hang vertically. In trying to get her leg back from the hip, she has made herself stiff.

This rider has taken her stirrup back but pushed her legs too far forwards. The stirrup leather is not hanging vertically but is pushed forwards.

Benefits of riding without stirrups

If you keep on practising without stirrups in small amounts, you will soon feel some positive benefits. Your balance will improve, your seat will become deeper and your legs will become longer. Indeed, you will probably be surprised that after only a few minutes' riding without stirrups when you go to take your stirrups back your legs will feel quite short. If this is the case, well done! You have kept your thighs long and your hips soft. You may even need to let the stirrups down a hole, depending on how short they feel.

However, if you or your riding instructor feel that you cannot let the stirrups down yet, then be careful not to move back in the saddle to make room for yourself – this puts you behind the horse's centre of motion and will be of no benefit.

Although riding without stirrups can boost your confidence and help you progress to bigger and better things, most riders use them when they are out hacking.

Making progress

Once you feel confident about riding without your stirrups in walk and trot, you are well on the way up the horse riding ladder. And as your confidence increases, you will be able to ride for longer without stirrups and start to control your horse without any assistance. You will find that you can ride school figures and stay in balance with your horse. As he turns left, you will follow him rather then hoping that you do not wobble and, more by luck than by judgement, go with him. When those words 'Quit and cross your stirrups' are said, you will no longer quake; you will just get on with it and use the opportunity to improve your riding position, balance and feel of what is going on underneath you. You are well on the way to becoming a better rider.

want to know more?

• For a comprehensive list of books that will help you with suppling and fittening exercises, in addition to sports psychology, click on the BHS bookshop website: www.britishhorse.com

6 Tacking up and untacking

As you progress with your riding, you may wish to know more about looking after horses. Equine language is a minefield and can be very confusing for the uninitiated. It is useful to know the names of the parts of the saddle and bridle as well as how to put them on. If you wish to become involved with helping to tack up and untack your horse, discuss this with your teacher. Once they know you are serious, they will usually be happy to allow you to arrive early and tack up before your lesson.

Learning the basics

Undertaking basic stable management tasks will improve your confidence around horses. You can take stable management lessons rather than picking up knowledge on an ad hoc basis.

must know

Types of headcollar
A leather headcollar is always safer than a nylon one. If the horse gets caught up on anything, a leather headcollar will break and release him.

Carrying the saddle and bridle

If you carry the saddle and bridle correctly, then everything is less liable to get in a muddle. You should always put the headpiece of the bridle and the reins over your shoulder and the saddle over your arm with the pommel facing towards your elbow. If you ever have to put the saddle down on the ground, do make sure that you put the pommel towards the floor and bring the girth up so that it rests between the wall and the cantle to prevent it becoming damaged.

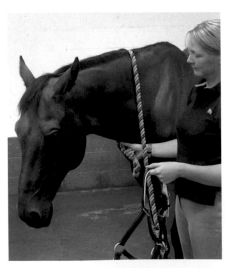

1 Put the rope round your horse's neck. This will give you a basic form of control.

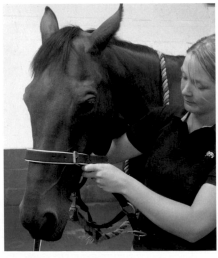

2 Stand facing forwards and quickly lift the noseband over the horse's nose.

You can put the saddle over the stable door, but this is not advisable until your horse is securely tied up. He may well knock the saddle from the door, leaving it with a broken tree and the riding school with a large bill for repairing it, or even replacing it with a new saddle.

There is a correct way to carry a saddle and bridle. It keeps the tack safe and prevents you from tripping over anything.

Putting on the headcollar

To put on your horse's headcollar, go into his stable with the headcollar and rope. Walk up towards his shoulder, talking gently and patting him. Put the rope round his neck, then put his nose through the noseband of the headcollar. Lift the strap over the back of his ears and buckle up the headcollar, so the noseband is two fingers' width below the protruding cheek bone. Always fully do up the buckle, so there is no danger of it coming undone. Check that the horse's mane is comfortable at the poll.

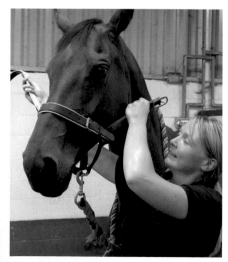

3 While holding up the headcollar, lift the headpiece over his head behind the ears.

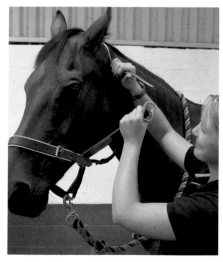

4 Buckle up the headcollar securely, making sure that it is neither too tight nor too loose.

Tying up a horse

It is very important that you know how to tie up your horse securely. You will need to do this every time you do something with him, whether he is to be groomed, tacked up or tied up outside his stable.

must know

Which method?
You should always use a quick-release knot, and there are two accepted ways of doing this, as shown here. Some riding schools prefer using one safety knot to the other, but others do not mind which one you use.

Quick-release safety knots

To tie up a horse, gently take the rope from round his neck and look for the tie ring on the stable wall. There should be a piece of breakable string attached to the ring and this is what you tie him up to. It is safer to tie him to a piece of breakable string, so that if he panics for some reason, the string will break and the horse will not damage himself.

1 Start off by making a loop about halfway down the rope.

2 Thread the loop through the string attached to the ring on the wall.

3 Make a loop with the loose end. Pull the rope through the loop.

4 Now thread the spare end of the rope through the new loop.

Alternative method

1 Start off by putting the loose end of the rope through the string.

2 Make a loop with this piece of rope close to the string.

3 Put this loop across and on top of the other part of the rope.

4 Hold the loose end near the loop; pull it through the loop to make a 'U' shape.

5 Now you should pull the rope really taut. Check that it is not loose.

6 Put the loose end through the loop to complete the quick-release knot.

Putting on the bridle

Putting on a bridle can be made to look very easy indeed when it is done by an experienced person. However, it is quite a complicated procedure and one that you must learn to do yourself.

must know

The right order
When your horse is tied up, remember to put the saddle on the door where he cannot reach it to knock it onto the floor. When tacking up, it does not matter whether you put on the saddle first, or the bridle. Just make sure the horse and tack are safe while you do so. If using a martingale (see page 185), put the bridle on first or otherwise undo the girth to attach the martingale to it.

Seek expert advice

If your horse is helpful, it is much easier to put on a bridle, but if he does not want to assist you, it can be very difficult. As you are still learning to tack up, it is essential that a knowledgeable person is present to help and advise you when you are putting on a bridle.

Gaining confidence

If you are confident when you are working around horses, the more they will recognize this and respect you. Having an experienced horseperson present will help to boost your confidence and ensure that you undertake the task in a manner to which the horse is accustomed. If you adopt the routine he is used to, he will be more co-operative and relaxed about it all. Always remember that a horse is a creature of habit, and he will be happier with familiar processes that he understands.

Practice makes perfect

It is easy for a horse to lose his confidence and start getting difficult when he is having his bridle put on. Banging the bit on his teeth, inadvertently poking him in the eye or forcing his ears under the headpiece can all lead to a horse becoming worried. However, don't let this put you off trying to put on his bridle. With assistance, you will soon become competent.

Opposite: This horse's bridle is fitted correctly. If he is to be tied up, the reins must be twisted and put through the throatlash. The headcollar can then be put on over the bridle.

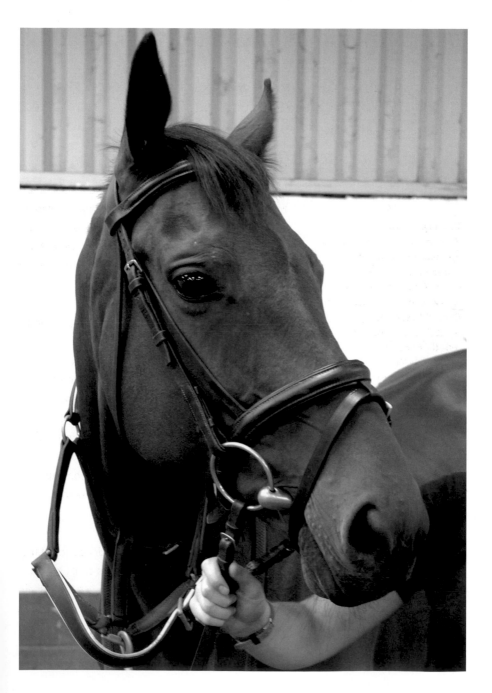

Putting a snaffle bridle together

1 To assemble a snaffle bridle, take the browband and then fold it the way in which it sits on the horse.

2 Slide it through the headpiece in such a way that it is forward of the throatlash on the right.

3 If at all possible, always hang the bridle from a hook, and then attach the cheek pieces.

4 Make sure that the bit is the correct way round and then attach it to the cheek pieces.

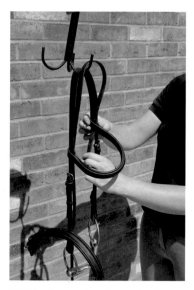

5 Now you can thread the noseband through the inside of the browband and the headpiece.

6 Take the noseband up under the headpiece and then down through the nearside of the browband.

7 The next step is for you to do up the noseband on the left-hand side (nearside) of the bridle.

8 Lastly, attach the reins to the back of the bit. Buckle fittings on reins face outwards; bits inwards.

The correct fit

It is essential that the bridle fits correctly – both for your horse's comfort and your safety. A well-fitting bridle should not be too large nor too small, too loose nor too tight. You can check the fit by carrying out a few simple

1 Undo the quick-release knot and leave the end slipped through the string. Put the reins over your horse's ears

2 Undo the headcollar and slide it down his neck before doing it up again – by doing so, you will still have control of your horse.

3 Put your right hand under his chin and reach round, so your hand is in the middle of his face. Hold the bridle at the cheek pieces in the right hand.

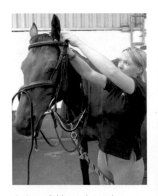

4 Bring the bit up towards the teeth. Put your left thumb in the side of his mouth. As he opens it, pull up the bit with your right hand.

5 Now keep on pulling the bridle up, and then you can gently ease the headpiece of the bridle over the horse's right ear.

6 As quickly and gently as you can, put the headpiece over the left ear, so that the bridle is now secure on the horse's head.

checks. There should be 5mm (¼in) between the side of the horse's mouth and the bit. Your hand should fit sideways under the throatlash. If you can't put a finger into the noseband, it's too tight. Two fingers should fit between the browband and the horse's head.

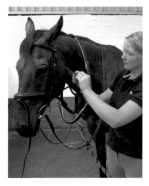

7 Pull the forelock out from under the browband, making sure that his mane is flat under the headpiece. Now you can do up the throatlash.

8 Ensure that the throatlash is not too tight. You should be able to get a flat hand's width between the horse's cheek bone and the leather.

must know

A horse's mouth
You may react with horror to the idea of putting your finger in a horse's mouth, but he has a gap between his incisor (front) and molar (back) teeth. This is where the bit sits comfortably, and you will not get bitten if you place your finger there. Don't put it in the bottom/front of his mouth – that is asking for trouble!

9 The noseband should be done up so you can get at least one finger between his nose and the leather. Check that the noseband is straight.

10 This bridle has a flash strap that does up under the bit, helping keep his mouth closed. The buckle should be away from the mouth.

Putting on the saddle

Putting on a saddle is not as complicated as a bridle, but you will still need an expert to assist you the first few times. Make sure that the girth is looped over the seat of the saddle or through the offside stirrup, so it doesn't flap around and hit you or the horse.

must know

Saddle tips
• If you are too strong when you are pushing the saddle into place, it will slide back too far. The withers should sit under the pommel and the saddle should not sit back on the loins. If you sit on a saddle that is too far back, it can damage the horse's kidneys.
• Do not slide the saddle forward if it is too far back – you will rub the horse's coat up the wrong way and may give him a sore back. By putting the saddle forward and sliding it back, you are going with the lie of the coat.

Numnahs

A numnah is a pad used under the saddle to relieve pressure and absorb sweat. Once the saddle is on the horse, check the numnah is pulled up under the gullet and is visible all the way round the saddle. If it presses on the withers or the saddle pushes on its outer border, it can cause painful pressure points on your horse's back.

Different numnahs can be attached to saddles in a variety of ways. Some, like the one shown here, may have no points of attachment, but you should attach them if there are the fittings to do so – this will help to stop the numnah sliding back under the saddle, which is uncomfortable for your horse.

1 Always put the numnah on a little further forward than the position in which you finally want the saddle to be. Do make sure that it is positioned equally on both sides of the horse.

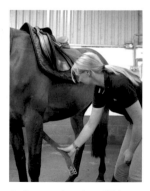

2 Take the saddle in both hands and lift it up so that you place it on top of the numnah. Again, it should be a little further forwards than the final position (as shown below in picture 7).

3 Pull the numnah up into the saddle's gullet. With the heel of your palm, push the pommel down and back until the saddle stops at the point where it sits correctly on the horse's back.

4 Go round to the offside of the horse and pull down the girth. Now go back round to the horse's nearside and bring the girth round under the belly and back up towards the saddle.

5 Buckle the girth up on the first and third straps. Only do the girth up tight enough that it will not slip round the horse's belly or too far back, and it will make the saddle secure.

6 Frequently, you may find that as you do up the girth the numnah will crease up. If this happens, it must be flattened out so that it does not cause a pressure point on the horse's sides.

7 You can see here that the girth lies in the correct position just behind the horse's elbow. The numnah has been straightened out and is still pulled up under the gullet of the saddle.

Untacking

To untack a horse, it is probably better to take the saddle off first, but, again, there is no hard and fast rule about this. You can do whatever works best for you and your horse.

Taking off the saddle

Always make sure that you have the headcollar to hand – if you are unsure, you might want to tie up the horse first. After you've taken off the saddle, it may be necessary to brush or wash any rub marks. Tell the staff if you notice any of these.

1 To take off the saddle, lift up the saddle flap and then undo both girth buckles.

2 Do not let the girth drop; the buckles may hit a leg. Put the girth down gently.

3 Slide the saddle and numnah back and lift off with both hands. As you do so, put them over one arm.

4 Reach for the girth with the other arm and put it over the saddle. Put the saddle down safely.

Taking off the bridle

When you take off a bridle, it is essential that you are extremely careful not to catch your horse's teeth with the bit. As with all things when dealing with horses, you need to be confident and efficient.

Be patient

Be patient as you take the bridle over the ears. Let it down slowly over the horse's face and wait for him to open his mouth to allow the bit to come out. If you are in a hurry and do this too quickly, you may knock his teeth, and the next time you do it he may react anxiously and throw his head up.

A little patience on your part can help to prevent a bad habit forming in the future. Remember to praise your horse and give him a pat to reward him for letting you ride him and for being patient.

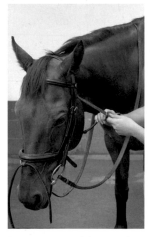

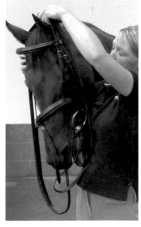

1 To take off the horse's bridle, you should start off by undoing the noseband together with the flash strap if there is one.

2 Your next task is to undo the throatlash. Having done this, you can then bring the reins carefully up to the horse's poll.

3 Stand facing forward and put your right hand under the horse's jaw. Reach for the headpiece and gently lift it over his ears.

Looking after tack

Tack should be cleaned regularly and your riding school may appreciate your offering to clean the tack you have used if it is not going to be used again that day. A strip clean involves taking the tack apart and thoroughly cleaning it. This should be done at least once a week but not necessarily after every ride.

Cleaning tack is not everybody's favourite job, but it is essential to keep your leather saddles, bridles and the other pieces of riding equipment in good condition.

Cleaning the bridle

Firstly, take the bridle apart and, with some warm water and a sponge, wash the leather parts without getting them too wet. This gets rid of all the dirt and dried sweat. Meanwhile, the bit should be left in a bucket of water to soak to ensure it is completely clean and ready to go into the horse's mouth the next time it is used. You would not want to eat with a dirty fork, and a dirty bit is not pleasant for a horse. If there is any congealed waste on the bit, it can give him a sore mouth. Dry it with a towel.

Once you have washed off the leather, you will need to saddle soap each individual piece. Take another sponge and dampen the saddle soap. Some people do this by spitting on the soap, while others dip the bar quickly into water and then shake off the excess. It is very important that the soap is not too wet, as you do not want it to lather up. Rub the sponge on the bar and then transfer the soap on the sponge to the leather. Remember always to soap both sides of the leather.

When you have soaped all the parts of the bridle thoroughly, it is time to put it together again. If you want to do a really good job, you will need to metal polish the buckles first, but do not put any metal polish on the bit. It is no mean feat to put a bridle back together and it is best done in a set sequence as already shown (see page 102).

Cleaning the saddle

To clean a saddle, the basic principles are the same as for cleaning a bridle. Take the stirrup leathers from the saddle and put the stirrups in a bucket of water to soak. The numnah and the girth (if it is synthetic) should be taken off and put in the wash. Wash the saddle with warm water, without getting it too wet, starting by soaping it underneath and then working towards the seat so you don't get finger marks on your hard work.

Make sure that you soap right up in all the areas that are hard to reach. However, only put a small amount of soap on the seat; too much will come off on the next person's jodhpurs.

Longevity and safety

A clean saddle and bridle will look and feel great, and they will certainly lengthen the life span of the leather. Usually there is not time to strip clean your tack every day, so just wipe it over with a soapy cloth. Removing the bridle parts from their keepers will help to ensure that all the leather is treated.

The tack you use at your riding school may not be perfectly clean, but it should be supple and well cared for – it should never appear hard and brittle with cracks in it. This can be unsafe and the tack may break under pressure, perhaps leading to an accident. Tack that is well cared for shows that the riding school cares for your welfare as well as that of their horses.

A well-maintained and tidy tack room is a vital part of a well-run school. All tack should be cleaned regularly and in good condition.

want to know more?

- *The British Horse Society Complete Horse and Pony Care* (Collins) gives you information on looking after tack. Other books on stable management are available from the BHS website at: www.bhs.org.uk
- Visit the tack shops in your area and talk to the specialist staff. By looking at a wide variety of tack you can start to understand its uses.

7 Refining your riding skills

How do you feel about your riding lessons? Are you looking forward to the next one? Does each lesson seem too short? Are you feeling confident about the skills that you have acquired so far? If the answer to all these questions is 'yes', then it sounds as if you are making good progress and enjoying your riding. However, if your answers are 'no', you need to sit down and think very carefully about your equestrian future.

Making riding more enjoyable

If you are keen to ride but do not feel happy about what you are doing, maybe your riding school is not right for you. Discuss your feelings with your teacher to see if they have any suggestions. If they are unable to help, then consider trying another school. It could be the change you need to move you forward.

must know

SMART goals
Discuss the goals you set with your coach. They must be SMART: specific, measurable, achievable, relevant, and time limited. Making sure that both your long-term and short-term goals are SMART will help your progress and motivation as a rider.

Building confidence

If you are still feeling nervous, you should discuss this with your instructor, too. Some novice riders are anxious because they do not feel secure on the horse. However, if you work hard on improving your riding position, this will help you to move forward and increase your confidence as a rider. It is never pleasant to feel unsafe and out of control, and a good instructor will be able to help you to improve your skills and overcome these feelings.

Work within your limits

Do not be worried about discussing your feelings honestly with your teacher – a good instructor will be able to understand and advise you. It is vital not to let anybody try to convince you to progress faster than you feel is within your limits, as this is where problems and doubts can occur about your ability as a rider. Like all other sports, there is a major psychological element within riding, and you must feel content mentally and physically if you are to become confident and competent. Ultimately, you are aiming to achieve a state of perfect harmony with your horse, where you are in tune with each other and respond appropriately.

Opposite: This horse and rider are in perfect harmony. The horse is listening to the rider and moving forward; the rider is focusing on where she is going. Her hands are too wide apart but she may be trying to ride forward and straight.

Learning to canter

It is especially important when you start to learn to canter that if you do not feel ready, you should not let anybody convince you to 'have a go'. Confidence is vital for success in learning this skill.

must know

On the right rein
When we talk about inside and outside legs, we are referring to the way in which the horse bends his body. With early riding exercises going round the school clockwise, the horse will incline to the right. The right rein will be on the inside of the arena, and thus the horse is said to be on the right rein.

Be prepared for cantering

As in all the other aspects of learning to ride, it is essential to have a horse who knows his job and will help you to learn. Mentally, cantering is a big step up and you will have enough to think about without having the 'wrong tools for the job'. Even when you are ready to learn to canter, you may still feel a bit apprehensive, although if you are well prepared, this will be outweighed by your desire to try.

Making the transition

When a horse makes a transition to canter, he moves from the two-beat pace of the trot to a three-beat pace. Consequently, the movement created by the horse is completely different to that of the trot. There are two ways in which a horse can make the sequence of three beats, and when he is in a manège he should always be cantering with the 'leading leg' being the same as the rein he is on. This sounds rather complicated, but if your horse is experienced, he will be balanced enough to strike off with the correct leading leg for you.

Beat numbers one, two and three
To canter in a manège, the first leg that the horse puts down is always the outside hind leg. An easy way to remember beat number two is to think:

'Beat number two is two legs together'. This is the diagonal pair of legs – inside hind and outside fore.

The third beat is created by the only other leg yet to be put down – the inside front leg. This beat number three is also called the leading leg and looks as if it is leading your horse forward because it comes furthest forward.

1 The horse's outside hind leg is the first one to be put down on the ground and starts the right lead canter.

2 The diagonal pair of legs, inside hind and outside fore, come forward and down together to make beat number two.

3 The inside fore leg is the last leg to be put down by the horse to create beat number three. This is called the leading leg. It should be the inside front leg when in a manège.

4 The horse is just about to take its weight from the inside fore leg to create a brief moment of suspension before the inside hind leg steps under to start the sequence again.

Notice that this rider is on the left rein. Her right leg is on the outside of the manège and she has moved it back into position to ask for the left lead canter.

Suspension

After beat number three, there is always a moment of suspension when all four of the horse's legs are off the ground together, and then the outside hind leg starts the sequence again.

Mastering the aids

The aids to make your horse canter are a little more complicated than any of the other aids you have used before, and although eventually you will need to be able to do these by yourself, you will probably find initially that your teacher will help you to make your horse canter by using their voice.

The transition to canter

You will be asked to make your transition to canter in a corner of the school. It is best if you try to do this in the first corner. If it does not work, you have the opportunity to try again in the second corner. The first time you canter, it will only be for a few strides to get the feeling. It is usually best if you hold the reins in your outside hand and hold on to the front of the saddle or the neckstrap with your inside hand.

As you approach the corner, you need to take sitting trot. It is now that you should put the reins into one hand and hold with the other hand. Your inside leg asks your horse to go forward into canter by nudging where it is on the girth, but your outside leg has to move back behind the girth to nudge. Remember that the leg that starts the canter is the horse's outside hind leg, so by moving your outside leg back as you use it, you are encouraging your horse to initiate the canter with this leg.

Stay upright

As your horse makes the transition into canter, he is likely to move your upper body forward and then throw it back. It is very important that you try to maintain the upright position you have learned to adopt in the walk and trot.

Try to follow the movement of the canter with your hips, and imagine that your bottom is trying to polish the saddle. In theory, you should just let the horse move your hips and you follow this, but at first it may be easier to move your hips a little from back to front of the saddle in time with the rhythm of the canter. This is not your long-term goal.

You will often see people 'scrubbing' the saddle with their hips in the canter – this is an indication of tension and tight muscles and is uncomfortable for the horse. When you start to canter, however, you will not be accustomed to the movement, so a little tension will automatically be there and you might as well use it to help your seat to stay in the saddle.

Basic mistakes

You will probably have made one of two basic mistakes. The most common one is to allow your upper body to collapse, so you bounce in the saddle as your upper body weight comes in front of your horse's balance. The next most common problem is that you will pull too much on the hand that is holding, so your weight goes behind your horse's balance and your legs are pushed forward. This may feel safer than being collapsed in front of your horse, but it makes it difficult for him to carry you and you will not be able to give any aids correctly with your legs too far forward.

must know

Class lessons
In class lessons there may be times when you all trot together. When learning to canter, you won't be asked to canter together as a group. You will do it individually. Although cantering with other people can be exciting, you must be proficient, safe and able to control your horse.

This horse is falling on his forehand as he goes into trot. He looks 'downhill'; his shoulders are lower than his hindquarters. The rider is trying to compensate by leaning too far back, with her legs pushed too far forwards.

Here you can clearly see that the horse's left front leg is the 'leading leg', coming furthest forwards within the canter.

Here the rider is a little tense because she is bracing her feet in the stirrups. Her reins are rather long, pushing her hands wide and low to maintain a contact.

Coming out of canter

You will probably only canter just a few strides on your first few attempts, and your horse should come back to trot with the aid of your teacher's voice and his experience of doing the job.

Going from canter to trot

As your horse comes back to trot, try to sit a couple of strides, then pick up your rising trot and come back to walk. You will then need to readjust your position, get your breath back, have a discussion with your coach and have another go.

To ask your horse to go from canter to trot is similar to the way in which you ask him to go from

This rider is comfortable in canter, riding in harmony with her horse, although note how her hands are thinking backwards.

Notice how this horse is relatively well balanced. This means that he is prepared to make a better downward transition.

trot to walk. You sit up a little taller, keep your legs on the horse and feel with both hands on the reins. You can use your voice and ask him to 'te-r-ot' in a long, soft voice. Try to stay upright and do not allow the transition to throw you forward. You don't have a seat belt to keep you secure, so tighten your body a little to compensate. The more upright you keep your body, the more you help your horse maintain his balance. This, in turn, means that your balance will not be thrown by him falling on to his forehand.

Rider and horse interaction

The interaction between you and your horse is a continual process and you will influence each other. This is why, when you are learning to ride, you need an experienced horse who can keep his balance even when you are wobbling around on top of him.

As you progress and your riding improves, you will feel how your balance can influence your horse, but this is something to aspire to in the future.

The best way to learn

The only way to learn to canter is to get out there on a horse and just do it. Until you experience the movement for yourself first-hand and how it affects your body, you will not progress.

Some riding schools have access to a mechanical horse, which can start to give you the feel of the canter but with less stress, so that you are more prepared for the real thing. Eventually, however, you will have to get on a horse and do it yourself if you are to become a better, more proficient rider.

The horse has moved into trot and, though he is a little downhill, he is much better balanced, so the trot can swing forward.

Improving your canter

The only way to improve your canter is to practise cantering. Do it in short bursts, so you can constantly correct your position. Gradually, as you become accustomed to the transition and the movement, you will become more confident and relaxed.

Balance is important

As you learn to maintain your balance with your horse, you can keep hold of both reins. As your balance improves, you can start taking control of the canter – the horse will canter when your aids ask him without the assistance of your teacher.

School figures

You will start performing school figures in canter; a 20m (6oft) circle is the first one you will learn. You will also canter across the diagonal, say, on the left rein from F to H (see page 82). As you are going to change the rein, you will need to trot somewhere or you will end up on the wrong leading leg as you go round the school. Practise asking for your trot at different points along the diagonal, say, just before H or at X. To be able to ride your horse from trot to canter and back again is a major step forwards. Also ask for smaller circles down to about 15m (45ft).

Different horses

When you are happy in canter on one horse, start trying others. Each one has his own rhythm and stride to the canter, and some move very smoothly from one pace to another while others can seem to 'jump' from trot to canter.

1 Here an experienced rider is turning to come across the diagonal on the right rein in right canter.

2 The horse and rider come across in canter, and as they cross the centre line the horse is asked to trot.

3 The rider establishes the trot, making sure it is well balanced, going forwards and straight towards letter K (see page 82).

4 The rider asks for left canter; the canter lead is correct as they go onto the left rein. This is called a simple change through trot.

Riding transitions

Transitions are the key to good riding and, as you progress and wish to improve your horse's way of going, they are one of the best ways of achieving this. If you can ride a smooth transition, keeping your balance and helping your horse to keep his, then you will see an improvement in both of you.

must know

The half-halt
As you progress as a rider, you will be able to help your horse and let him know that you are going to ask him to do something before you do it. This is called a half-halt. It uses your legs, seat and hands in combination to a greater or lesser degree to say to your horse: 'Listen to me, balance yourself. We are about to do something different.'

What is a transition?
A transition is a change of pace, either between or within paces. An upwards transition is from a slower pace to a faster one, whereas a downwards transition is from a faster pace to a slower one. A progressive transition is where a horse moves progressively through the paces, e.g. from walk to trot to canter. A direct transition is where a pace is omitted, e.g. from walk to canter. You will learn how to ride this later on in your riding education.

Performing a good transition
To perform a good transition, your horse must step under his body with his hind legs. In so doing, he transfers more of his body weight onto these legs, making his forehand lighter. When he does this, he is more pleasant to ride because he is not so heavy in your hand. It is also easier to control him because he is more balanced, and can respond to your aids more quickly.

The aim of schooling
A horse will naturally carry about 60 per cent of his body weight on his forehand, and 40 per cent on the hind legs. One of the main aims of schooling

him is to try and change this balance by building up the muscles of his hindquarters and encouraging him to step under with his hind legs so he can take more of his body weight behind.

Ideally, we would like the horse to carry at least 50 per cent of his body weight on his hind legs, and the more advanced his schooling becomes, the more we are trying to get him to carry something nearer 60 per cent of his body weight behind. This is obviously a long-term aim but one that is well worth striving for.

Riding good transitions is one of the best ways to achieve this goal. At a more basic level, we need to be able to ride good transitions so that we can control our horses.

This horse is 'hollowing' his body as he goes into trot. His head is coming up high and he looks rather unhappy. The rider may be using too much hand.

Improving your feel

It will take a great deal of practice to ride good transitions. Whereas some horses may require positive aids, others may respond to only very subtle ones. Part of your equine education is to improve your feel, so that you quickly realize how responsive the horse you are riding is. As you progress, this will become easier because your 'feel' will improve. Most riders will find this very motivating and will want to 'feel' more.

It is always a good sign if you are starting to feel what your horse is doing. It means that you are developing a more relaxed approach to your riding and the tasks are becoming more automatic, so that you don't have to think about them so much. Consequently, you are able to think about other things, such as feel. When this happens, you are well on the way to becoming a good rider.

want to know more?

• Watch experienced riders to observe how smooth everything looks and whether there is harmony between the horse and the rider.
• There are many good instructional DVDs that can give you useful tips and information. For details of these, go to: www.britishhorse.com

8 Hacking out

When you feel confident about cantering and can maintain good balance with your horse, you are ready to take a major step forward. What most riders look forward to is hacking out. This can be really good fun, relaxing and exhilarating, but it may be something you feel apprehensive about initially. Do not worry if you have that sinking feeling about hacking out. Just as when you learned to canter, do not let people push you into something that you don't feel ready for. Only you will know when the time comes to try hacking out.

Your first hack

The first time you hack out, your riding school may decide that just you and your instructor should go out together. This is less daunting than venturing out with a group of riders, but it may not be possible, depending on how busy the riding school is.

This horse and rider are easily visible to other road users. Notice the two fetlock bands, which are positioned on the outside legs.

Keep it simple

If you feel that you are ready to go out for a hack, discuss this with your instructor first. They will know the area and the hacks that are available. Your first hack should be as uncomplicated as possible, with easy terrain and routes that are relatively enclosed. It is always best to hack out on a horse that you have already ridden. This will help to boost your confidence as you will know and trust him.

However much you are looking forward to escaping from the confines of the riding school, a one-hour hack is probably long enough for your first venture into the outside world, as this is the length of time that you would normally ride in a lesson.

Clothing

When hacking out, always make sure that you dress appropriately for the prevailing weather conditions. For example, if it is raining, then it is important to have a waterproof jacket – there is nothing more miserable then getting soaking wet. However, if the weather is fine, warm and sunny, try not to be tempted to wear a sleeveless or strappy top. It is always advisable to ride with your arms covered, even when it is hot, so that if you should be unfortunate enough to fall off, your arms will be protected and thus you will not damage the skin. Otherwise you are advised to wear normal riding wear (see page 23).

High-visibility clothing

If you have to go out on to the road during the course of a hack, it is strongly recommended that both you and your horse wear high-visibility gear. Reflective bands around your horse's fetlocks are extremely effective as drivers tend to look down towards the kerb when they are driving. A tabard and light-coloured gloves for yourself are also useful and will help to attract other road users' attention.

must know

Where to ride
Hacking out is great fun and a good way to see the countryside. The BHS *Where to Ride and Train* lists centres in the UK and overseas where you can go out hacking. Beaches and open spaces are many riders' idea of perfection. Fresh air, good company and a horse are a recipe for riding happiness.

This rider is wearing light-coloured gloves, so other road users can see her hand signals more easily. If you carry a whip when riding on the road, hold it in your right hand to help keep your horse to the left side of the road.

Hacking guidelines

Before you start your hack, your riding instructor will run through a few basic rules and guidelines with you. For Health and Safety reasons, it is vital that you do your best to observe them.

School regulations

Different riding schools will have different regulations, depending on the number of people out on the hack and the terrain you are going over. If there are three or four of you going out together, then there will probably be an assistant for your instructor who will ride at the rear. They will be able to keep a careful eye on what is going on and will be able to assist you if there are any problems.

Mounting up

You will probably mount up in the stable yard and will be put in a riding order that will suit the horses. Once you are mounted, make sure that your girth is tight and that your stirrups feel comfortable. If you

These riders have mounted in the yard and are going out on a hack that does not involve road work. Some riding schools, but not all, may insist that you have your arms completely covered.

These riders are riding in single file and are keeping a sensible distance apart. They are not too close to the horse in front to get kicked, but not so far away that their horses may become worried about being left behind.

have developed a fairly long length of stirrup for riding in the school, you may well be advised to shorten your stirrups a little. Ask your instructor what they think about the length of your stirrups; they will be able to advise you.

Two abreast or single file?

Your teacher will let you know how they want you to ride. Sometimes riding two abreast is suitable, while at others you will be in single file. If you have to go on the road, then try and keep well to the left-hand side. If you carry a whip, make sure this is in your right hand; it will help to keep your horse to the left.

Cantering

If you are enjoying your first hack out and are feeling secure and confident, you may be given an opportunity to have your first canter outside. This

must know

Riding and Road Safety Test
If you are going to hack out regularly, it may be advisable to take The British Horse Society's Riding and Road Safety Test. This is a very useful educational experience and will give you advice on how to ride safely on the road. Your instructor will give you details of the Test, or you can contact The BHS Safety Office (see page 187).

This horse and rider are enjoying an exhilarating canter up a hill. For many people, there is no better way to relax and enjoy their riding than to go out into the countryside for a hack.

These riders out on a hack are riding two abreast. The horses are used to this and are behaving well. They do not think that it is a race, and they are not nervous of each other. They are swinging along in a forward trot.

will give you a real sense of achievement and may well feel easier than when you do it in the school because you will be travelling in a straight line and your horse will find it easier to balance himself.

Be prepared and alert

When you are out hacking, you must always be prepared for the unexpected. Do not be tempted to ride along on a loose rein, totally absorbed in gossip with other riders – there is always the possibility of something spooking your horse. Even the most unflappable of horses can be frightened by a stray plastic carrier bag being blown towards you or by a pheasant flying up from behind a hedge.

Remember that horses are creatures of flight; in the wild, if they are frightened by anything, they would rather run than stay and fight. They will only resort to fighting if they are cornered. However, if you can successfully negotiate hazards, it will help to increase your confidence and improve your balance, thus making you a better rider.

Improving your balance

Riding out over hills and rough terrain will help to improve your balance. If you are going up a steep hill, incline your body slightly forward, keeping the weight into your heels. This will help the horse to get up the hill and be great for your balance. If you feel you are unable to keep your weight forward, hold a piece of mane or the neckstrap to help you.

When riding downhill, do not lean too far back. Keep your weight in to your heels and think of sitting upright. The steeper the downhill gradient, the more you need to think of 'leaning back'.

want to know more?

- **The BHS Safety Office can give you information on how to hack out safely. Telephone them on: 01926 707782.**
- **Contact the BHS Access Department on 01926 707781 for more information on hacking routes and bridleways throughout the UK.**
- **You can also log on to the BHS website at: www.bhs.org.uk**
- **For tips and general advice on hacking out, see the specialist equine magazines (see page 188).**

9 Learning to jump

Just when you are starting to feel confident about your riding, your instructor will throw something else in to test you. How about learning to jump? You may well have similar anxieties to the ones you had when you were learning to canter, or going out on your first hack. Remember those feelings and how you overcame them – you can do the same with jumping. Every rider should learn at least the basics of jumping. Many horses love to jump, and you will discover that it really is fun.

Preparing to jump

Initially, when your teacher broaches the subject of learning to jump, you may well feel that jumping is not something you really want to do, but it is always useful to have at least a basic knowledge of jumping, so that if you come across a log or a ditch when you are out hacking you have the ability to get to the other side.

Use a reliable horse

Do not let anyone push you into learning to jump, but you should be prepared to have a go when your instructor thinks that you are ready. Many people feel that jumping is one step too far for them, but an all-round horse person should be able to jump, even if it is only over very small obstacles.

It is very important that you are taught to jump on a reliable horse. Your favourite might not enjoy jumping, so you may have to use another horse.

This rider is shortening her stirrups ready for jumping. She is doing this incorrectly as she has taken her feet out of the stirrups.

This rider has a secure position for jumping. Her weight is pushed down the back of her leg into her heel to give a strong lower leg.

Feeling secure

There are two main reasons why many people don't enjoy jumping. Some are taught to jump on horses who are not reliable over a fence and are thus unsure as to how they will get to the other side safely. Others do not enjoying jumping because they have not been taught correctly, so the riding position is insecure. When a horse jumps, he transfers his weight to his hindquarters, pushes down to give himself spring, stretches out over the jump, lands on his front feet and brings his hind legs under him.

Consequently, you, the rider, need to be able to follow this movement, and to make this easier for yourself, you may need to shorten your stirrups. The number of holes depends on several factors. Your instructor will help you get the correct length.

Jumping positions

The classic jumping position is where the rider adopts a fold through the hips, and to become a competent and confident jumper, you will learn to adopt this position.

The light seat

Before you start to jump, it is important to become secure in the 'light seat' position. Within the horse world, there are several names for this position – some people call it the forward seat, others the poised position, but whatever name you use, they are all the same thing. There is also a great deal of discussion as to whether these are all the same as the 'jumping position'. This is not something for us to get bogged down with here, but you should discuss all this with your riding instructor, so that you are both talking about the same thing.

This rider is becoming more insecure as his lower leg slips further back. He needs to work to keep his weight into his heels.

Your lower leg

As you will discover, the most important part of your light seat is your lower leg. This is actually your anchor, and if it stays underneath you, supporting your body weight, then you will be very secure when you are jumping. If your lower leg comes back, you will tip forwards; and if it is pushed too far forward, your body weight will be pushed back behind your horse's point of balance.

Shorten your reins

You should shorten your reins in the light seat position because your hands need to move forward a little along the line of the reins towards your

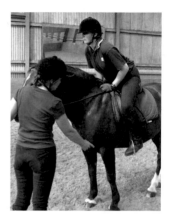

This rider is not pushing her weight down into her heels. She is insecure and rests her hand on her horse's neck for balance.

This rider has allowed her lower leg to slip back too far, and, consequently, she has collapsed onto her horse's neck.

Notice how this rider's stirrups are a little too long, and thus he is trying to stand in the stirrups rather than fold.

horse's mouth. Do not reach so far forward with your arms that you push yourself out of balance, but if your hands are a little forward either side of your horse's neck, they will follow the stretch of his neck and not interfere with his motion. Nothing puts a horse off jumping quicker than being pulled and restricted in his mouth.

1 This rider is practising the light seat in the canter, and is working on undulating ground.

2 Notice how she is completely in balance with her horse, with a secure lower leg.

3 Here you can see how the horse and rider are both focused on what they are doing and are looking forwards.

4 On the third beat of left canter, the rider still has a secure lower leg, although her knee is just a little tight.

Take it gradually

As a novice rider, you must be secure in your light seat in all paces before moving on to pole work and jumping. This is not something to be rushed; it has to be worked for and practised. You will probably feel some pulling in the tendons and the ligaments down the back of your legs initially when you start working on your light seat. Why not ask your instructor if you can rest your legs by taking them out of the stirrups for a minute or two at halt – this helps relax your legs.

Your upper body

Your back should not collapse and become rounded as you incline forward a little from the hips. As has been discussed earlier, the amount that you incline your upper body forward can differ for different body

These riders are working as a ride in the indoor school. They have all shortened their stirrups in order to practise their light seat work.

To stretch out the back of your legs, stand with the balls of your feet on the edge of a bottom step and then push down on your heels.

This rider is riding over a single pole in the light seat. Her upper body is balanced, but her reins could be a little shorter with the hands towards the horse's mouth.

shapes, and as long as you are secure and remain in balance that is all that matters. You should look between your horse's ears, and don't forget to smile!

Practise in halt

You need to practise the light seat in halt until you can find your balance easily and feel secure. You may well feel a stretch down the back of your legs. An exercise you can do to help this is to stand on the balls of your feet on a step or the bottom stair and push down on to your heels. Do this a few times, then rest and repeat. A simple exercise of touching your toes will help to stretch the back of your legs.

Practise at walk

When you are happy that you are able to maintain your light seat in halt, you can move on to trying it

at walk. As soon as the horse moves, however, you may have to readjust your balance to stay with him. Do not pull on the reins to balance yourself.

Notice how this rider has lost his balance as his lower leg slips back. His reins are in loops as he has had to rest his hands on his horse's neck to balance himself.

If you have a neckstrap, it should be a high one, which is positioned around your horse's neck where your hands should be. However, if you do not have a neckstrap, then hold the mane, although this does encourage you to put your hands up the horse's neck rather than following the line of the reins. Do not hold this position for long periods, as you can quite easily strain yourself.

Practise the trot and canter

Once you can balance yourself in walk, then it is time to try the trot. In this position, it is better not to do rising trot, but to hover a little above the

This rider is trying to make sure everything is correct and is very tight and tense. She just needs to relax more and keep on practising.

This rider is working in balance over three trotting poles. The horse looks happy and is working in harmony with the rider.

saddle. Make sure that your weight stays down into your heels, and your knees and hips stay soft, so you can absorb the horse's movement. If you thought the walk was difficult, then the trot will be even more so! Again, it only takes practice in small amounts to build up your feel and body fitness.

Needless to say, once you have managed the trot, you are ready to move on to the canter. Try to give your aids for canter in the light seat, rather than sitting down and then taking the position again. By the time you are efficient in the trot, you will not find the canter too onerous, although giving the aids in light seat is relatively difficult. It is hard work but worth it for the security that you will achieve in your jumping.

Practise over trotting poles

The next step is for you to practise your light seat over some trotting poles. Your riding instructor will probably put out a single pole first for you to get the feel of it. Your horse may lift his legs a little higher as he goes over them.

This gives you more movement to absorb and helps you stay in balance. It is accepted practice that if the trotting poles are placed in such a way that there is not a stride between them, you go from one pole to three. This is so that your horse does not get confused and think that he has to jump them. You will practise going over single poles and lines of poles in various parts of the school. Some may be on the long side and others across the diagonal, which helps to improve your balance. Going round corners and turns in the light seat is the next step.

Starting to jump

By now you should be very secure and the weight should stay down in to your heels without you particularly having to think about it. At this stage, you are ready to move on to actually jumping.

Your first jump

It may have seemed a slow build up to jumping, but by doing it this way you ensure you are safe. Time spent practising your light seat is never wasted.

must know

Through the ears
When learning to jump, try to keep looking through your horse's ears all the time. If you look down, it collapses your body. If you 'duck' to the left or right, it can upset your balance and affect your horse's way of going. If you feel the need to 'duck' to avoid the horse's neck, you are folding too much.

This horse and rider have approached the middle of the cross pole and are jumping it in good form. They are both looking forward and are jumping straight over the middle of the jump.

Your first jump will normally be a cross pole with a placing pole in front of it, so your horse reaches the jump at the correct point for take off. This jump is inviting for you, the rider, and the horse and has the advantage of encouraging you to jump in the middle.

Approaching the jump

Your first jump may well be executed from trot. It needs to be active, but not running. However, if you can feel and create the right pace for your horse to go over the trotting poles actively, then that is the approach pace you will need to adopt for the jump.

Going over the jump

Take up your trot and light seat and make a good approach turn, so you are heading for the middle of the fence. Stay in your light seat, and take hold of the neckstrap or mane and keep your legs on. Your horse should help you out by maintaining the same rhythm over the placing pole and then over the fence. Keep breathing with your weight in your heels, and do allow yourself to collapse as your horse lands on the other side.

Try it a few times

Your horse may well only treat the jump as a high trotting pole, but do not worry if this is the case as it will give you the opportunity to get to the other side of a jump without making too much effort.

Congratulate yourself that you have done it – and safely, too. Once you have accomplished this a few times, you can start to breathe as you go over the fence and also begin to think a little more about what is going on.

1 This horse and rider have taken the placing pole in canter, but the rider is confident and secure and is not disturbed by this.

2 They are still in harmony as the horse jumps the cross pole from canter. He should only do this if he is asked to canter.

1 This horse and rider are approaching the placing pole in trot. However, the trot could be a little more forward.

2 The horse is going over the placing pole. The rider should have adopted a light seat by now in order to stay in balance.

3 The horse takes off over the cross pole. The rider is holding the neckstrap, so as not to interfere with the horse's mouth.

4 The horse lands after crossing the fence and helps the rider by continuing forward in a straight line.

Five phases

A horse's jump always consists of five phases:

- The approach
- The take off
- The flight
- The landing
- The getaway.

The getaway can also be the approach to the next fence if you are jumping more than one obstacle. The horse should be obedient and in balance through all phases of the jump.

A person who is learning to jump should never be asked to ride a horse who is not established in his jumping, or doubt can enter the rider's mind. A novice jumping horse and a novice rider do not go together.

1 This pair are approaching a fence in canter. The rider is in balance with a light contact on the reins, looking forward. The horse is looking at the fence, keeping his rhythm and balance.

2 Notice how the horse is arriving at the fence and preparing to take off and jump it. The rider is not getting her body weight in front of him, but is waiting for him to take off over the fence.

3 The horse is undertaking the second phase of the jump: the take off. The rider's lower leg should be a little more secure.

4 This is the third phase of the jump: the flight over the fence. Both the horse and rider are looking forward.

5 The fourth phase of the jump is the landing. The rider's lower leg is very secure here. Some riders, especially novice ones, tend to collapse when the horse lands.

6 Here you can see the fifth and final phase of the jump – the getaway. Although this horse and rider are not approaching another fence, they could do so if they wished.

Learning from others

Jumping is not an easy skill to learn. The problem is that three of the five phases of the jump - the take off, flight and landing - all happen very quickly and they are not always the same.

On take off, the rider has lost the rein contact, and her lower leg could be a little more secure.

This rider has lost rein contact but she is in balance and riding positively forward. Both horse and rider look happy and secure.

Watch other riders jumping

When you are learning to jump, and even when you are more proficient, practising the skill can be quite difficult. If you watch people jumping, this will help you to progress. You should not worry if you cannot achieve a perfect jumping position and maintain total balance with your horse every time he jumps. The most important thing is not to use your reins to help you to balance – this is the job of your lower leg. As you become more proficient, you will stay in balance with your horse more easily, and as your feel and confidence improve you will really start to enjoy your jumping.

Over the flight of this fence, the rider's lower leg is insecure, so she has to rest her hands on the horse's neck to balance herself.

As this rider takes off, she is pushing her upper body too far forward over her hands, so her elbows are sticking out.

1 Above: You can see here how the rider is making a good approach in balance to the fence to be jumped.

2 Below: The rider tries to take off before the horse, but her balance is too far forward, making it difficult for the horse to take off.

3 Above: Because the rider's lower leg is secure, she is able to take the fence safely and land without too many problems.

4 Below: The rider is approaching the fence again, but this time she remains in balance at take off.

Perfecting your jumping

Once you are happy and confident about going over a fence, your job as the rider is to get your horse to the fence in rhythm and balance. His job is to get you safely to the other side.

Landing in canter

When you feel competent jumping a fence from trot, try to approach it a little more positively. Aim to land in canter and then canter away from the jump. If riding in a manège, your coach may put a second fence on the other side of the school, so you land in canter, canter round the short side of the school, maintain the rhythm and positive feel to the canter and then approach the second fence. You have now jumped two linked fences together and also jumped from canter – a major step forward.

It sometimes feels easier to jump from canter, but as you progress you may worry about 'seeing a stride' to a fence and forget to ride forward. Instead, try to maintain a good canter. If the quality is good – purposeful and balanced, taking you forward but not rushing – your horse will arrive at the fence correctly. It is only when you jump over 1m (3ft) high that you need to think about 'seeing a stride'.

Circle before you start to jump

Get into the habit of cantering at least one circle before you approach the first jump, so the canter is positive. You can't do this for every fence if you are linking some in a course, but part of the skill of jumping a course is maintaining the quality of the canter, especially when you are going round corners.

One stride double

When you can link two or three fences together spaced out around the manège, and you are able to maintain your balance, guide your horse accurately and help him to maintain his rhythm, the time has come to start thinking about jumping fences closer together.

There are various types of closely linked fences: a double, a bounce and a related distance. These fences can also be linked together to form gridwork.

The easiest type of linked fences to jump is a one stride double. This is where your horse jumps one fence, takes one stride of canter, and then jumps a second. Your teacher will probably get you to jump the first fence a few times and then put the second one in for you. You may be asked to approach the first fence in trot and then land in canter, or you may approach in canter. It will depend on your horse and your level of competence. Your teacher may then put a third fence in for you to jump in a line.

This horse and rider are jumping the middle of the fence. The rider is in balance with the horse, and they are both looking forward. The rider's position is secure, and they both appear to be enjoying themselves.

1 This horse and rider are approaching the first element of a one stride double fence.

2 Both horse and rider focus on the middle of the fence and are committed to the jump.

3 As they prepare for take off, the rider just gets in front of the horse's balance.

4 The rider realizes and balance is regained, but the horse takes off a little right of centre.

5 The horse and rider focus on the second jump. The rider's lower leg slips back a little.

6 As they land, they both look at the second fence and are committed to going forward.

7 The horse brings his hind legs to the ground and the rider stays in balance.

8 The horse takes a stride of canter. The rider is maintaining good rein control and security.

9 The horse takes off at the second fence. This time he is positioned at the middle of the fence.

10 The rider's balance is a little forward but does not interfere with the quality of the jump.

11 The rider shows a good lower leg and balance, but her upper body is a little round.

12 The getaway shows that they could move on to another fence if necessary.

Gridwork

There are many different combinations of fences that can be used to vary the number of strides between fences and the number jumped. Gridwork is fantastic for your jumping position, balance and suppleness. The fences are set up so that everything happens easily and the horse will take you through the grid once you are in.

Benefits of gridwork

Gridwork has many benefits for the rider. The fold through your hips will improve as will your feel and the way you follow your horse's movement. Your lower leg will become more secure and your hands and arms will follow the stretch of the horse's head. However, in spite of all these advantages for you, gridwork is hard work for your horse, so you will have to be content with only going down the grid a few times each lesson.

1 This horse and rider are approaching a three-jump grid. The first jump is a cross pole. This is to encourage straightness and to make it more inviting for you to jump.

2 The horse has landed and is looking at the next fence. This gives the rider a positive feeling of going forward. The horse knows his job and is focused on the next fence.

3 The horse brings his hind legs underneath him and then moves forward into the one non-jumping stride. He is still helping the rider by thinking forwards.

4 The horse takes the non-jumping stride. The rider must be very careful to follow the movement of the horse and not to try to anticipate the next jump.

5 Here the horse is preparing to take off for the second fence. This is a simple, inviting upright fence. The rider is anticipating the take off a little too much.

6 The horse takes off. The rider needs to ensure that her lower leg stays secure under her body. She is becoming a little tense; her face gives this away.

7 The horse lands safely and shows that he is not necessarily focusing yet on the next fence. Notice how the rider's leg is secure and is keeping her position safe.

8 The horse has now seen the third fence as his hind legs come under him. Notice how the rider is in good balance with the horse, and the horse is keeping his rhythm.

9 The horse takes the one non-jumping stride again. Note that the rider is just a little in front of the horse and needs to correct her position. Her hands are helping her balance.

10 The horse is now preparing to take off at the third fence, which is a simple spread fence. The rider's balance has been regained and is good as they approach the fence.

11 The horse takes off over the fence. The rider has exaggerated her fold. This may be due to the fact that this fence is a spread. Consequently, her hands are resting on the horse's neck.

12 The horse is stretched out over the spread fence. Both the horse and rider are positive. The rider has regained her balance and you can see that she is very secure.

13 The horse and rider land safely after the third element and have performed well through the grid. The rider is showing empathy and has not disrupted her horse's ability to perform.

14 The getaway shows that both are thinking positively and enjoying themselves. Occasional loss of balance through the grid has not been so great as to be detrimental to the horse.

Jumping a bounce

When your instructor tells you that they are going to put up a bounce for you, either as part of a grid or by itself, then you should feel very proud of yourself indeed – you are jumping well and are making excellent progress. A bounce is where your horse jumps a fence, lands and then takes off again for the second fence.

This exercise is extremely hard work for your horse, and, as such, he will put a great deal of energy into jumping this exercise. Consequently, he will move you, the rider, more than he will for a double or for a series of fences making a course. However, as long as your lower leg is secure when you are jumping a bounce, you will be able to absorb the movement and go with it.

If you can achieve this, you are justified in feeling satisfied with your progress as you are now well on your way to becoming an extremely competent jumper. Like all aspects of riding, you will need to practise your new skills regularly in order to improve and fine-tune your jumping.

Taking it further

If you feel like progressing with your jumping, discuss this with your coach. Once you feel secure and confident jumping in an enclosed area, you might like to try jumping some fixed fences or 'cross country'. Not all riding schools have this facility, but it can be really challenging and enjoyable. Remember that your lower leg is absolutely vital when jumping on variable terrain, so make sure you are using it properly. Ask your coach's advice on how to do so.

Opposite: A happy partnership of a rider and her horse obviously both enjoying their jumping.

want to know more?

- Some good DVDs are available that will help you to understand the technique of jumping. Look on the BHS website at: www.bhs.org.uk
- All the monthly horse magazines feature regular articles on how to jump and improve. See the following websites: www.yourhorse.co.uk www.thehorse.com www.horseandrideruk.com

10 What if something goes wrong?

As with any other sport, when you are learning to ride sometimes things can go wrong. Riding is an activity where you have another living, thinking being that you have to take into consideration – your horse – and this is one of the reasons why you may have the odd bad day. Remember that any rider, no matter how experienced they are, will encounter problems sometimes that they need to overcome.

Earn your horse's respect

Your horse may not always be on the same wavelength as you. He may come out of his stable and feel off colour, or come in from the field having been pestered by flies and thus be tired. This is why, as a novice, it is useful to ride the same horse as often as possible, so you can build up a relationship with him.

must know

Good relations
It is important to build a relationship with the horse you are riding. If you do not gel with the horse, why not ask your teacher if you can try another one instead? As with people, there will be some horses you do not get on with.

Well-schooled horses

The better schooled your horse is, the less he will let his moods affect his way of going, but, just like a stroppy teenager, there may well be days when you seem to be unable to get the horse on your side. As you progress with your riding ability and

This horse and rider are tuned in to each other. Their mutual trust is such that they can tackle a grid of fences and appear at ease.

your confidence grows, these days will become fewer as your horse will respect you more and will not feel that he is able to ignore you.

A good riding school will keep the horses used by novices 'tuned up', with the staff schooling them regularly, hacking them out and possibly taking them to competitions. This will help them to stay generous and assist you rather than ignore you. Although it is better to ride the same horse until you feel confident, if you feel that your horse is starting to take advantage of you, discuss this with your coach and see if you can try another horse.

One reason why your horse may ignore you is that you are being asked to undertake tasks on him that you are not yet capable of achieving. For example, you may be asked in a group lesson to ride your horses past the rear of the ride. Your horse may decide he is going to stay with his friends and, if so, you will be unable to make him do what you want.

Here the rider is riding past the rear of the ride. This may sound an easy exercise, but with the horse's herd instincts, he will want to go to his friends rather than past them.

Lunge lessons

If your riding aids are not sufficiently well coordinated or strong enough to undertake an exercise like passing the rear of the ride, you need to work on improving your position and core stability. The best thing to help with this is to have some lunge lessons, so that you do not have to worry about controlling your horse.

must know

Stiffness
If you have difficulties trying to work towards a correct, in-balance position, it may be due to stiffness. Indeed, many people turn to other forms of exercise in an effort to increase their suppleness and flexibility. Yoga, T'ai Chi and The Alexander Technique have all proved useful for riders with stiffness problems. One of them may suit you – you can only try.

Concentrate on your position

You can work on your depth of seat to improve your core stability and security. As a result of this, you will find that if you ask your horse to do something and he disagrees, then your position will not be compromised. You will be able to maintain enough balance and strength of position to be able to tell him quite positively that you want him to obey you. A lunge lesson makes this easier, as you can focus on your position without worrying about control.

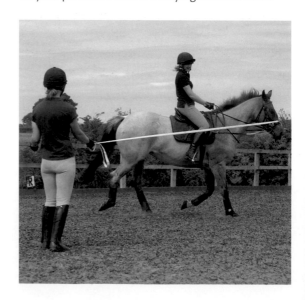

This rider is having a lunge lesson on a well-mannered horse who is used to this type of work. This helps her to concentrate on her position while the coach controls the horse on the lunge rein.

Using a stick

Once you have an independent seat and do not use your hands to help yourself balance, your instructor may suggest that you try riding with a stick or whip to help back up your aids.

Reinforcing the aids

When you have mastered the art of carrying and using a stick, a horse who is prone to ignoring your leg usually becomes more responsive and respectful of your aids. Riding school horses, especially, tend to know when you are carrying a whip and can be transformed into paragons of obedience. However, some horses will not tolerate you carrying a whip; these are usually the more sensitive ones.

Many people feel that a stick is cruel, and in the wrong hands it can be. Whips tend to be used to remind a horse that he has to listen to your leg. Consequently, when you give your horse a leg aid you firstly give him the opportunity to respond. If he does not react, then the second time that you use your leg, do it in conjunction with your stick. Use the stick as close to your leg as possible, so the horse connects the two. Hopefully, the next time you use your leg, he will respond to it immediately without the use of the stick.

Types of stick

There are two kinds of stick you can carry: a short whip, which is used for jumping and hacking out, and a schooling whip, which is longer and is used for flatwork. The short whip is easier to hold and control but it is more difficult to use correctly.

When you are carrying any whip, be it long or short, it should go through your hand and rest across the middle of your thigh. Do not rest your thumb on the stick; this will stiffen your hand.

must know

Types of whip
There are many
different makes and
styles of whip. If you
are going to purchase
one, discuss with your
teacher which length
will be best for you and
the horses you ride.
Always buy a whip
that has a weight and
balance that suits you.

Using a short whip

When you are riding in a manège, usually you should carry your whip in your inside hand to ensure that your horse is listening to your inside leg. This is the dominant leg, which is telling him to go forward by motivating his inside hind leg.

To use a short whip, you will need to put both your reins into the hand that is not holding the stick. This is so that you can move your hand back to use it behind your leg. If you don't do this, you will be pulling your horse in his mouth as you use the whip. You would then be telling him to stop and go at the same time – a recipe for confusion.

Changing the whip over
When you change the short whip over when changing the rein, it does not matter where you do it. Just choose a convenient place that will not upset your horse's balance or way of going. This may be after the corner when you have changed the rein. Some people maintain that you must change the whip as you go across the diagonal, but this is not the case.

The whip should always be held
through your hand and positioned
between the thumb and first finger.

1 To change the whip, put both the reins into the hand that is holding the stick.

2 Pull the whip through over the horse's withers and in front of your body.

It is only practice that will make you efficient at changing the whip over. At first, you will be a little clumsy, but do not give up. You will find that you are more comfortable holding the stick in one particular hand. You need to ensure that you are happy carrying the stick in both hands, but, again, this will come with practice and experience.

Using a schooling whip

To use a schooling whip, all you need to do is learn how to flick your wrist and hand in a quick sideways movement. Your hand stays still, so there is no necessity to put your reins in to the other hand. Think of turning your little finger in and up a little in a short, sharp movement. This will move your hand and forearm and make the end of the whip flick on to the horse behind your leg. Initially, you may find that you catch yourself with the whip, but don't worry – you will soon learn the technique.

must know

Schooling whips
A schooling whip tends to be used only when you are riding in a manège. You are not allowed to compete in jumping competitions with a long whip. If you are planning to compete one day, you will have to learn how to use both types of whip.

Changing over a schooling whip

This is a different process from using a short whip. The whip is too long to bring through in front of you, so you will need to learn the technique that is illustrated below. There is more than one way to change a schooling whip, but the one shown here is probably the easiest.

1 Start by putting both the reins into the hand that is holding the stick, as you would if you were changing the short whip.

2 Turn the hand so the thumb goes down and the whip turns up. Turn the other hand, so that the thumb is also turned down.

3 Take hold of the whip in the new hand and turn your hand back to the normal position.

4 Now put the reins back into both hands. You have smoothly changed the whip over.

Falling off

Falling off is obviously not something that any horse rider enjoys and, although the likelihood of it happening can be minimized, there is always a possibility that it can occur.

Health and Safety

If your riding school has good Health and Safety processes in place and they work with you at a pace you feel comfortable with on horses who are suited to the tasks you are undertaking, then there is less possibility of you hitting the ground.

Do remember, however, that horses are living, thinking beings who are creatures of flight, so there is always the potential for something unexpected happening. Horses may trip over violently or shy suddenly at something that has caught their eye, and that might be all that is needed for you to lose your balance and fall off.

Get back on again

A fall can easily shake your confidence, and it even may make you question whether or not you wish to continue riding. If you have a fall and are definitely not injured, sometimes it helps to get straight back on the horse, even if you just walk around a little afterwards. If you feel that you do not want to get back on, that's fine – do not let anyone push you into it. Discuss with your instructor the reason for your fall and how, if possible, it could have been avoided. Talking it through with someone will help you to rationalize what happened, which, in turn, can help you to come to terms with it.

must know

Not for you?
If, after falling off, you feel riding is definitely not for you, then don't be afraid to admit it. Not everyone enjoys skiing or playing tennis, so it is not compulsory to enjoy horse riding. However, it is advisable to try again one more time after a fall before giving up completely.

Don't be disheartened

Try not to let a first fall put you off riding. Give it another go and take the pressure off yourself by doing some basic exercises in your next lesson. If you still feel nervous and worried, you can take heart from the fact that most other people feel the same the first time they ride after a fall. In fact, it may well take more than a single lesson to start enjoying yourself again.

Lost your nerve?

Many riders find that their desire to be with horses and their pleasure in riding them will eventually overcome their worry about falling off. If you really want to continue with your riding, but have 'lost your nerve', either from falling off or for some other reason, then try spending some time looking after horses: mucking out, grooming them and cleaning tack. Just being with them can help to build up your confidence again. Do not try to hide your worry – it will never get better like that.

Your teacher will help

Discuss it with your instructor and explain how you feel. They will encourage you to continue and take you back as far as you need to go. Even if you have to go all the way back to having your teacher walk round with you, there is no need to feel that this is demeaning. As long as you continue to work at a level you are happy with, you will soon feel your confidence returning. It will not be long before you get fed up with walking round and want to move on to something a little more exciting and challenging.

Saddle comfort

Some people find it extremely difficult to be truly comfortable in the saddle. Saddles come in many shapes and designs, but you will probably learn to ride in a general purpose saddle which is a compromise between a jumping and a dressage saddle.

Maintenance and safety

Saddles are extremely expensive items to purchase, and it is important that they are looked after carefully to keep them in good condition. Not only must they be cleaned regularly (see page 111) but they should also be put down correctly. They should never be left on a horse's back without the girth being done up, as he could shake himself and the tree (see page 186) could break if the saddle lands on the ground. So try to take good care of the riding school's investment.

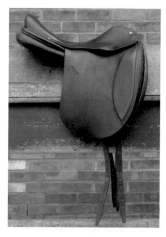

A dressage saddle has a fairly straight flap in front of your knee, often with long girth straps, so the buckles aren't under the knee.

The general purpose saddle is a compromise between the dressage and jumping saddles. It is a little more forward cut than a dressage saddle but not as much as the jumping saddle.

A jumping saddle has a more forward knee roll and a flatter cantle, so that your seat can move back in your jumping fold.

The right saddle
Do not feel as though you are always asking your teacher questions or trying to monopolize their time. They should be prepared to discuss things with you and make adjustments if possible. A different saddle that fits you and the horse can make a huge difference to your security and position.

This rider has very long legs and he will encounter difficulties finding a suitable saddle in which he can feel comfortable.

The right fit

The saddle you use must primarily fit the horse. If you are riding at a riding school, many different people will use the same saddle, but if you have your own horse, you can ensure that the saddle will fit both the horse and yourself. If you always feel uncomfortable in the saddle, then talk it over with your instructor. It may be too small or too big for you. If it is too big, you may well feel insecure; if it is too small you may feel very uncomfortable.

Of course, it may not be possible to find another saddle that fits both you and your horse, but if you change horses the new saddle could be just what is required and you will feel more comfortable.

Checking your stirrup length

You may not always feel comfortable when you're learning to ride. You will be using muscles that you have forgotten you had, and there will be pressure on various parts of your anatomy. Your seat bones are a real pressure point, and you should always be able to feel them both equally when you are riding. If you cannot do so, check your stirrups are level.

Level stirrups
This may seem obvious, but it is surprisingly easy to get in to the habit of having one stirrup longer than the other, and eventually you will think that they are level. Once you become a competent rider, your instructor may not check that your stirrups are level for you, and you will have to do it yourself. If the school has a mirror, take a look in that to see. Get into the habit of checking both stirrups against your out-straightened arm before you mount.

Above: This saddle is too small. The rider's bottom is almost off the back of the saddle.

This saddle fits both the horse and the rider. The rider can sit comfortably in the middle with room to move if necessary.

must know

A good position
Most problems stem from an insecure, poor position. Check your position every time you ride, even if you are only hacking out. We all need to be checked regularly.

Checking the length
Another way to check your stirrup length once you are mounted is to check the position of your knees in relation to the knee roll of the saddle – are they both the same distance from the knee roll and do your knee joints feel bent the same amount? Counting the holes in the stirrup leathers is an

This rider (above) is not straight. Note how the left stirrup is longer than the right one. The rider (right) is level, with her weight distributed equally on her seat bones and the stirrups level.

unreliable way of telling whether they are level, as leather can stretch different amounts.

No excuses

As with jumping length stirrups, flatwork stirrups will alter for each individual rider, depending on their anatomy, the horse's size and the type of saddle they are using. People with very long thighs or lower legs may well have to compromise their riding position, but there is no excuse for not having their stirrups the same length. This must always be checked, whether you are just riding round in a school or manège, out hacking or jumping.

Are you one-sided?

When you are sitting in a chair or driving your car, see if you can feel both your seat bones equally. You may well have a tendency to lean to one side without even knowing it. If this is the case, think about the way you are sitting even when you are not on a horse. You may be surprised to learn how one-sided you are, and this will have an effect on the way your horse moves.

Mirror check

Another way to check that you are sitting level is to sit in front of a mirror and look at your shoulders. Are they level? Look at people on the television and around you – observe how many people do not sit with their weight equally distributed, so their shoulders are not the same height. It is not just a problem that you have. However, as a rider who wants to improve, you need to work on improving your posture and weight distribution.

This rider has a good stirrup length for performing any flatwork. Notice how the stirrup leather is hanging vertically. The rider appears to be comfortable.

This rider's stirrups are too long for the depth of seat, and she is reaching for them. Consequently, her foot is insecure in the stirrup.

Practice makes perfect

Some people do not progress with their riding as quickly as they would wish, and this can be frustrating for them. Do remember that riding is a sport and, while books can give you some valuable guidance, there is nothing like practice to improve.

must know

Stay relaxed
Sometimes the more you try to analyse what you are doing, the worse it gets. This is because you try so hard that you lose your softness and do not listen to what your horse is trying to tell you. If possible, try to relax and listen to your instructor. We all have different learning styles, and some are more suited to riding than others.

Make an effort

It is possible to 'sit' on a horse and enjoy yourself, but you will never make genuine progress unless you put some effort in to what you are doing. This uses energy and takes mental concentration – just as in any new skill you choose to learn. Learning to ride is doubly difficult because there is another living being involved – the horse.

Be patient

Do not become frustrated if you do not feel that you are progressing as fast as you should. Riding well is an extremely difficult skill to master; in fact, many accomplished riders will tell you that they do not feel that they are a 'good rider' as there is always something new to learn. Nobody knows everything about riding and horses – this is one of the reasons why it is so fascinating. So keep an open mind and just go on practising – you will get better and better.

You will improve

As you gradually improve, your feel for what is going on underneath you will get better, and you will find you are starting to correct things your horse is thinking about doing before he actually does them. Although things will go wrong less frequently, there

This horse and rider are enjoying themselves, working well and practising together in a manège.

will always be the odd day when something does not work. Horses are not automatons and you must remember this. You will find that as you improve, you will gain more and more skills that will help you to build up a good relationship with any of the horses you ride. Then you will be well on the way to becoming an accomplished horse person.

want to know more?

- The BHS website has a list of Registered Instructors, some of whom may be prepared to discuss your problems with you. Go to: www.bhs.org.uk
- Look on the Internet to find equine website chatrooms, which may prove useful, but don't forget to talk to your riding school, too.

Glossary

Action The way in which a horse moves.

Bay Brown colour body with black mane, tail and lower legs.

Blaze A broad white stripe running down the face.

Cantle The back of the saddle.

Cavesson A piece of equipment made of leather or nylon worn by the horse when he is being lunged. The lunge line attaches to the metal ring on the nose piece.

Chestnut Ginger-red colour of the body and mane and tail.

Cob A weight carrying type of small horse, usually with a good temperament.

Concentrates Food for horses other than grass, hay or haylage. Often pre-prepared, ensuring a complete balanced feed.

Core stability The strength of the trunk area of your body.

Crib-biting A 'stable vice' whereby a bored horse grabs something with his teeth and takes in air.

Diagonal The way in which a horse moves in trot with opposite pairs of legs moving one after the other.

Diagonals In rising trot, the rider sits as the outside front leg and inside hind leg are on the ground.

Dressage The art of training a horse, so that he becomes obedient and responsive to the rider.

Dun Yellowish or cream body colour with black mane, tail and lower legs.

Equitation The art of horse riding and horsemanship.

Flatwork Working and schooling a horse where no jumping is involved.

Fold The position taken by the rider as the horse jumps over a fence.

Forehand Front part of the horse, including the head, neck, shoulders and forelegs.

Frog The 'V' shaped part of the sole of the horse's foot that acts as a shock absorber and helps blood circulation.

Gelding A castrated male horse.

Girth gall A sore area in the girth region, caused by friction or a dirty girth.

Grazing Grass fields for horses to live on and eat the grass down.

Grey Any colour horse from pure white to dark grey.

Grooming kit The various brushes and tools that are used to clean a horse.

Hack Going out for a ride.

Hand Traditional unit of measurement for horses and ponies, equivalent to 10cm (4in).

Hock Joint in the centre of the hind leg.

Impulsion Powerful, controlled forward movement.

Irons Stirrup irons attached to the

saddle by stirrup leathers in which the rider's feet are placed.

Kind eye The horse's eye looks gentle, friendly and interested in what is going on.

Knee rolls The front padded part of the saddle flaps. The knee lies behind them.

Livery An establishment providing paying accommodation for horses.

Lunge The horse works on a circle with the teacher holding a long lunge line attached to a lunge cavesson on the horse's head. A long lunge whip is held to encourage the horse forward.

Manège A purpose-built riding surface designed for use in all weather conditions.

Mare A female horse.

Martingale An attachment that goes through the girth and attaches to a part of the bridle to prevent the horse putting his head above the point of control.

Mucking out The daily task of cleaning out the stable, taking out the dirty bedding and making the bed tidy and comfortable.

Nearside The horse's left side.

Neckstrap A strap, usually made out of leather, that is attached round a horse's neck for a rider to hold should they need help with their balance.

Numnah A pad used under the saddle to help keep the saddle clean and absorb sweat, shaped to fit the saddle.

Offside The horse's right side.

Palomino A gold or cream coloured horse with a white mane or tail.

Glossary

Piebald A black and white horse.

Poached When fields are very wet, the area around the gateway and water trough becomes very muddy and churned up.

Points of the horse The names of each part of the horse.

Poll The point at the top of the horse's head immediately behind the ears.

Pommel Raised front part of the saddle.

Post Rising up and down in the saddle. This is usually in rising trot, sometimes done in the canter.

Quit and cross your stirrups Take your feet out of the stirrups and cross them over onto the horse's shoulders, so you can ride without stirrups.

Rising trot Action of the rider rising from the saddle in rhythm with the horse's trot.

Roan A colour produced from a mixture of white and any other coloured hair distributed over the horse's body.

Saddle soap Specially prepared soap to keep leather saddlery clean and supple.

Shy When a horse is 'spooked' by something and moves quickly to one side.

Side reins Two pieces of leather attached from the girth to the bit rings used when lungeing to help control the horse.

Skepping out (skipping out) The removal of droppings from the stable during the day to help keep the horse's bed clean and tidy.

Skewbald Any two-colour coat other than black and white.

Skull cap A form of riding hat that usually has a coloured silk over it. Often worn for cross-country jumping.

Snaffle The commonest type of bit that usually has a ring at each side. It is a mild bit.

Sock White pastern and fetlock.

Star A white patch on the forehead.

Strapping A complete thorough grooming of the horse.

Thrush A disease of the frog which is often associated with poor foot hygiene.

Transition The act of changing pace. From a slower pace to a faster pace is an upward transition. From a faster pace to a slower pace is a downward transition.

Tree The frame of the saddle to which the leather is attached.

Turn out To put a horse out in a field.

Weaving A 'stable vice' whereby a bored, stabled horse rocks his head and neck from side to side stereotypically.

Wind-sucking A 'stable vice' whereby the horse will gulp in air without grasping something with his teeth (*see* crib-biting).

Wisp A pad made from twisted hay that can be used instead of a massage pad to bang the horse when strapping.

Withers The highest point on the horse's back at the base of the neck. The pommel of the saddle fits over them.

Need to know more?

Useful organizations

British Dressage Ltd
National Agricultural Centre,
Stoneleigh Park, Kenilworth,
Warks CV8 2RJ
tel: 024 7669 8830
www.britishdressage.co.uk

British Equestrian Federation
National Agricultural Centre,
Stoneleigh Park, Kenilworth,
Warks CV8 2RN
tel: 024 7669 8871
www.bef.org.uk

British Eventing
National Agricultural Centre,
Stoneleigh Park, Kenilworth,
Warks CV8 2RN
tel: 024 7669 8856
www.britisheventing.com

British Horse Society (The)
Stoneleigh Deer Park,
Kenilworth,
Warks CV8 2XZ
tel: 01926 707700
fax: 01926 707800
www.bhs.org.uk

British Show Jumping Association
National Agricultural Centre,
Stoneleigh Park, Kenilworth,
Warks CV8 2RJ
tel: 024 7669 8800
www.bsja.co.uk

British Veterinary Association
7 Mansfield Street,
London W1G 9NQ
tel: 020 7636 6541
fax: 020 7436 2970
www.bva.co.uk

**Department for Environment,
Food & Rural Affairs (DEFRA)**
Nobel House,
17 Smith Square,
London SW1P 3JR
helpline: 08459 335577
fax: 020 7238 6609
www.defra.gov.uk

Endurance GB
National Agricultural Centre,
Stoneleigh Park, Kenilworth,
Warks CV8 2RP
tel: 024 7669 8863
fax: 024 7641 8429
www.endurancegb.co.uk

Need to know more?

Equipilates
8 Speedwell Cottages,
Milton Keynes MK17 9HT
email: info@equipilates.co.uk

Pony Club (The)
National Agricultural Centre,
Stoneleigh Park,
Kenilworth, Warks CV8 2RW
tel: 024 7669 8300
fax: 024 7669 6836
www.pcuk.org

Royal College of Veterinary Surgeons
Belgravia House,
62–64 Horseferry Road,
London SW1P 2AF
tel: 020 7222 2001
www.rcvs.org.uk

Society of Master Saddlers (UK) Ltd
Green Lane Farm,
Green Lane,
Stonham,
Stowmarket,
Suffolk IP14 5DS
tel: 01449 711642
www.mastersaddlers.co.uk

Trailblazers
PO Box 642,
Preston, Lancs PR3 3WZ
www.trailblazerschampionships.com

Worshipful Company of Farriers
19 Queen Street, Chipperfield,
Kings Langley, Herts WD4 9BT
tel: 01923 260744
www.wcf.org.uk

Worshipful Company of Saddlers
Saddlers' Hall, 40 Gutter Lane,
Cheapside, London EC2V 6BR
tel: 020 7726 8663
email: clerk@saddlersco.co.uk

Useful websites

Driving Standards Agency
www.dsa.gov.uk

Equitech Software Ltd.
www.equitechsoftware.com

Horse & Country TV
www.horseandcountry.tv

Horse & Hound
www.horseandhound.co.uk

Horse & Rider
www.horseandrideruk.com

The Horse
www.thehorse.com

Your Horse
www.yourhorse.co.uk

Index

Collins need to know?

Look out for these recent titles in Collins' practical and accessible need to know? series.

Ballroom Dancing

Calorie Counting

Cat and Kitten care

Detox

Digital Video

DJ Tips & Techniques

Dog and Puppy Care

Downloading

Food Allergies

Horse and Pony Care

Latin Dancing

Pensions

Running

Sleep

What to do with your Digital Photos

Other titles in the series:

To order any of these titles, please telephone **0870 787 1732** quoting reference **263H**. For further information about all Collins books, visit our website: **www.collins.co.uk**